I AM SOMEWHERE ELSE

*Gospel Reflections from
an Emerging Church*

Barbara Glasson

DARTON · LONGMAN + TODD

First published in 2006 by
Darton, Longman and Todd Ltd
1 Spencer Court
140–142 Wandsworth High Street
London SW18 4JJ

ISBN 0 232 52597 8

A catalogue record for this book is available from the British Library.

Designed and produced by Sandie Boccacci
Phototypeset in 10.5/13.75pt Palatino
Printed and bound in Great Britain by
The Cromwell Press, Trowbridge, Wiltshire

For the silent, the silenced
and all who wait for the word.

Contents

Acknowledgements

Someone once said that to live your life completely it is necessary to have a child, climb a mountain and write a book. So far as I am aware, they did not say that they were all the same thing!

From conception to delivery, there have been many who have been midwife to these words, who have fallen into step on the hard inclines. So, my thanks go to James Alison, Donald Eadie, Geoff Cornell, Ann Morisy, Brendan Walsh and all the staff at DLT for bringing this book to birth.

To the artist Kjell Walfridsson in Sweden, whose gift of painting, poetry and song-writing have emerged triumphantly from his own struggles. His picture on the front cover is called *The Seed*.

And to my family, past, present and future, in whose non-conformity I have been formed and nurtured.

But, mostly, thanks to the unexpected companions, especially the community that is emerging at 'Somewhere Else'. The abused, battered, silenced. Some who have risked a great deal in being named in the text. The rough-sleepers, addicts and troubled of the city, who reveal what it means to be generous.

So, this book is especially for everyone who thinks they are nothing, for whom life seems too barren or precipitous. That you too will discover, as I have done, the surprising companions of the word.

Introduction

This is a book about life and faith and whether these can still be connected to the church. It is a story of one community's attempt to live out of this question and some of the struggle and wonder we have encountered in the process. It is written not only to share our story but also to inspire you within your own. It is an encouragement to claim your own experience and in naming and relishing that experience to grow in the joy and contradiction of life and faith. I hope it will help you persevere and glimpse the possibilities of a different way.

Faith, like life, begins as a gift not a doctrine. I move, I breathe, I see, I relate, I love. Life dawns on us as we grow in self-awareness. We do not know why we are alive but with every breath we breathe we experience life as a given. Sometimes we are thankful for it and sometimes it scares us witless. I believe faith is about questions not answers. Questions that emerge from living the life-gift. How can I live with my fear? What does this relationship mean? How do I deal with my anger? Living out of our own questions is the way that we begin to get to grips with who we are and possibly to move on to ask some of the questions behind all existence, 'If life is a gift then who or what is the Giver?'

Of course most of us can avoid most of these questions for most of the time. It is probably only at times of transition that they hit us in the face and, because we have spent much of our lives avoiding them, it is at these moments we are most off balance and we are left asking questions when we most want to have answers. I believe that we grow most when we begin to live out of our own struggle. That living our own nonsense is the best place to engage with what it means to be human and that is where the church should be too – not in a doctrinal safe house but at the ragged edge of our contradictions and questions.

All this sounds rather grand. My reality was brought into sharp focus as I was driving along the M62 in a westerly direction one afternoon in late summer. I was somewhere between Leeds and Castleford having a conversation with God (no doubt the drivers around me were also having a conversation with God as I recall that I was not concentrating much on the road). The conversation I was having was going something like this: 'Help, what am I going to do about my new job?' I had just been appointed to Liverpool city centre as the Methodist minister, all of which sounds fine and ordinary until you realise that at that time there was no Methodist church building and no congregation. 'How am I going to make a church visible when it is invisible?' By the time I had reached my friend's house in Castleford I had a word buzzing through my mind, the word was 'bread' and at that point I could only begin to imagine why.

Six years on from that gift of imagination I look in wonder at the little bread-making community that now gathers in a kitchen above a bookshop in the centre of the city. There is no big sign that announces we are here; a small door with an intercom needs to be sought out in a row of shops. Usually there is a guy selling the *Big Issue* just outside. Each Tuesday and Thursday whoever turns up is welcome to make bread around a large table and, if they choose, to take some quiet time, to light candles and say prayers. It is a singularly unspectacular place and yet there is an extraordinary sense of genuine human encounter and surprise here. A puzzling place full of contradiction, wonder and struggle. We call it 'Somewhere Else'.

The inherited church has historically worked with a process of understanding faith that has used the tools of Scripture, reason, tradition and experience. The first three points of embarkation – Scripture, reason and tradition – assume a certain engagement with text and history. It is important that an emerging church such as Somewhere Else holds these things in mind, but for us the starting point for living out of our questions is experience not tradition, reason or biblical text. And I do not mean 'religious experience' but all experience, the ordinary stuff of being a human being, and we usually tell of this experience not through the written word but through narrative, through conversation, through jokes or anger. Bread-making as a process gives time and space for such conversation. It allows our experience to hang around with us, for stories to unfold and struggles to be shared. It gives time to 'experience our own experience'. That is, savouring what has happened to us, recounting the twists and turns of our day-to-day lives, enjoying odd moments in the company of others, sharing our struggles. This takes time and space and attention, a sense of safety, of holding and respect.

And this leads to questions. Personal questions like 'How am I real about my own anger, my desire for silence?' 'What does it actually mean to love people that I do not understand?' 'How do I challenge violence within myself?' Then there are questions about my faith: 'Can there be salvation when people are not safe? What does it mean to belong? What is the reality of forgiveness in the face of abuse?' And questions about the church: 'What are the hallmarks of an authentic eucharistic community?' 'What does it mean to honour and value diversity?' 'What is worship beyond words?' The dynamic these questions present is an energising one but pushes us to an uncomfortable place where no answers are sufficient. We are led to a place of 'yes, but . . .'. So Somewhere Else is essentially a transitional place. This 'yes, but' place has emerged as a dynamic and life-giving church albeit fragile and quirky.

So, I have discovered a desire to talk to someone about it all and decided to refer back to the Bible in the light of this experience. I am not looking to the ancient text for answers because answers seem to be culture-laden and can close down a discussion. On the contrary, I want to have the kind of conversation that holds questions alongside each other and lets the dynamic between them come alive. This is not to take huge leaps between biblical texts and the people around the bread table and draw some time-resistant conclusions. The Bible was written within a radically different culture and experience from our own. It is rather an attempt to let the voices speak one to the other and find that the echoes of the search for the Giver resonate between us. And of course I am drawn first to the author of St John's gospel who knew so much about transformation because, like us, he has been a witness to it, in a community of half-believers and around the struggles at the dinner table. And he knew a bit about bread too.

So, in the pages that follow you can eavesdrop on this dialogue. You will find it does not go in a straight line, it is a 'yes, but' conversation. There are moments when it sets off on some connection of stories and you have to hold tight to keep with the thread. You will be introduced to some people by name and to others by pseudonym. Constraints of confidentiality have led me to blur some characters and you may not receive as much personal description of people as you may feel you would like. Sometimes you will only get hints of what is going on – this is true for the Gospel too. You will not be able to wrap this story up and put a bow on top and say 'Aha there is a neat set of arguments that gives me the answers that make sense of my life and faith' – thank God. It is simply a look at the world and the church from Somewhere Else.

1
Mixing

꒰ ꒱

I am making bread. There is a warm smell of yeast bubbling enthusiastically with the honey in the jug. I write my initials in the flour with the oil. Then three spoons of salt disappear into the bowl. 'Don't you ever get tired of making bread?' someone asks. Truthfully I can answer, 'No'. It always fills me with excitement as I begin to pummel the glutinous mixture. The salt stings my hands. My fingers stick together. 'You have to go on believing in bread. You have to believe it knows it is going to be bread.' It does. Yeast and salt, oil and honey, warm water and malted flour combine to become elastic and smooth. They give each other life, texture, warmth and identity. Bread is full of wonder.

And so is the church of which I am a part. It began with a word. The word was 'bread'. This community has emerged after the closure of a big city-centre Central Hall. It has been named 'Somewhere Else', the Methodist Church Somewhere Else, but it is usually referred to as the 'bread church'. It is working out what it means to be a Christian community around the making, shaping and sharing of bread. I look around the table. Here is a wonder-full community of odd bods like myself. We have wandered here from many different experiences with a variety of different motives. Simon used to sell the *Big Issue*, Tony still does. Col had 'sacked the church' and stumbled on us by accident. Penny is transgendered and has brought a number of people with mental health issues.

Terry lives in a house run by the Independent Living Alliance. There is a student or two, Harry who is two years old and Ahmed who is seeking asylum. Some of this community are gay and have never felt really welcome in a church before. Some have been so abused that they have never felt safe anywhere, least of all in church. Others work and come to make bread to relax or think. This is the wonder of it.

More than that. This church has caused me to return to the gospels and re-examine what they might mean in a community such as this. How can we talk of salvation or holiness or Eucharist in such a way that it makes sense here? This is a challenge for me as I work alongside this mixed-up bread community. In reality it is the challenge for all people who still consider faith might be worth exploring. In particular I have returned to St John's gospel, the one in which Jesus describes himself as 'the bread of life'. I wonder what that means for us here and now and whether it can make any difference to the people of this place.

The bread is rising in the proving oven. Each bowl is different, marked with the baker's initials. Soon it will be shaped and rising again ready for baking. By the end of the morning there will be two loaves for each person and enough for lunch. It will fill our kitchen with such a delicious smell that other people will appear around the door to investigate. By two o'clock we will have completed our task. The tins will be returned to the cupboard. The people will disperse. Bread will be taken all over the place and given away. Heather and Andrew will take some to the office. Terry has a loaf for his community. Tony will deliver some to his regular customers. The bread tells its own story, holds its own wonder, brings its own delight.

The bread is not just a symbol of our community. We have become known as the bread church because the bread is shaping us; it is showing us how it is possible to be together as a gathering of completely random people on hugely different trajectories in life. How we can begin to meet face to face in our common humanity. It has also made us ask some sharp questions about what it might mean to be around the same table in God's company. How can we be safe here? How can we begin to value the huge diversity and complexity of each others' lives? How can we speak of a God who saves when there is someone on our doorstep who is in fear of his life? How do we emerge as counter-signs within a city centre with all its emphasis on commerce and trade? How do we trust the process of who we are becoming? You have to go on believing in bread. You have to believe that this mixed-up sticky mess will become something wholesome and nutritious. It takes a huge amount of energy and trust. But at the end of the morning we can see it with our own eyes. It is very good bread.

Mixing bread ingredients is a physical activity. It is hard work and gives you strong arm muscles. By lunchtime we will all be shattered. The dough needs to be stretched and pushed with the ball of our hands. We have to put our weight behind it. As we combine these ingredients we are enabling them to work with each other so that the yeast can feed on the honey and bring life to the lump of dough. Oil is needed to give texture and elasticity, salt slows down the fermentation and brings flavour. These ingredients change each other. They have to work with their different properties. They need time and warmth. Sometimes they require rest, at others they demand full attention and effort. To make good bread you have to understand how the different ingredients work together, their particular needs, their peculiar qualities.

So too with this community. We are a mixture of people. We each have our peculiarities and particular needs. In this way we differ from most other gatherings of people that tend to congregate around a common interest. This group of bread-makers has a huge variety of needs and skills and they represent a wide cross-section of abilities. Some of us are employed, some have never been employed. Some have university educations, others do not read or write, some cannot speak English. Some are married with children, some live in gay relationships with children, others are children. There's a granny or two and little Harry who has celebrated both of his birthdays with us. Penny has an interest in rallying vintage cars. We have people with anger-management issues and others afraid of men. Someone is claustrophobic as a result of childhood abuse. There's a Morris dancer, a folk singer and a lesbian who sings karaoke. There are those of us who are familiar with the ways of the church, others who have never been to church. There is a Muslim who has just been baptised and a woman abused by a priest. Some of us like to talk; others are shy and prefer to be left alone. Simon has his arm in a sling, three people are diabetic and one has epilepsy. Some come here to have some respite from what is going on at home, some come to escape from silence and loneliness at home, some have no home. And if I tell you that this community is only some thirty or so people in total then you will see that each of us is a mixture of all the above. Yet in other ways we are just the ordinary people that you come across from day to day. Each one of us is different and our lives are many-layered; even the most ordinary of people has a depth of human experience. Sometimes you see it and sometimes it is private and silent.

We bring to the bread table the mixed-up nature of who we are on this day. We bring our feelings and experiences. Tony has been selling the *Big Issue* for the morning. Someone has been aggravating him. It is quite common to be spat at and there is an uneasy relationship with some of the city-centre police. People know Tony. Terry's niece is expecting a baby and there are some complications. Terry is agitated and goes round and round the scenario with his carer. Little Harry is cutting a tooth.

This is how it is to be a human being. We are a mixture of all the things that shape us and all the things that impinge upon us this day. We are never the same person twice and when we mix in a community all that difference and complexity comes into play. There are not many places where it is possible to engage at this level with our humanity. Usually we gather into groups that expect us to be interested in only one part of us. We will go to the gym to exercise our physical body; we will go to a mental health support group to understand our schizophrenia; we will go to church to say our prayers. In this bread community we mix all of this together. We come as separate ingredients to community life. Some people will agitate others, some will bring delight. We laugh together and annoy each other. There are times when we make no sense at all. This is a community that works with all of that. That is why it takes a lot of energy. No wonder at the end of the morning we are shattered.

As we knead the bread dough we stand side by side around a large round table. The smell of bread is so evocative that it soon prompts people to remember stories. There might be memories of childhood or recent recollections of buying bread in a supermarket. Very quickly people are able to engage with times in their lives that are evoked by the bread. Smell is an active trigger to memory – rather like the tune of a song that we associate with one particular moment – so the smell of baking bread takes us straight to a visualisation of a particular encounter or occasion. As any hill walker knows, being side by side with someone else is an easy way to talk. There is a connection that is easier without the threat of eye contact. This conversation usually unfolds readily and can engage at different levels. It may feel safer at first to concentrate on the process of mixing the bread ingredients. As time goes on and confidence increases so some take the risk of sharing more.

This is not a therapy group. We are simply companions, which after all means 'together in bread'. Standing side by side is a physical manifestation of solidarity with each other. There is reciprocity in it. In its simple way making bread inspires an understanding of the radical equality of everyone. There is an inherent diversity in each of us that comes from within our genetics and our experience. As we hear people's stories so we are learning to honour the depth and nuance of that person. None of us tells a story that is without contradictions and paradox. Each of us speaks of how our lives have apparently taken bizarre twists and turns. This diversity is to be claimed as a rich source of wonder and growth. Meeting within this ambiguity contravenes a natural tendency to meet only with people we consider to be similar to us. The bread gathering is a group of radically different people. Our stories, our experiences, our way of looking at life are distinct. We have to find strategies for working within this difference. It can be hugely taxing but out of this struggle to be together come some wonderful moments of surprise. We are constantly amazed at the resilience of the human spirit and the ingenuity of the human mind.

This is a profoundly different approach from the model we see in most inherited churches. Rigorous doctrines or codes of behaviour mean that ambiguity is hard to hold in these structures. Encountering church around our bread table is uncomfortable and challenges us at every turn. In order to hold such diversity there is a need to enter into a way of being with each other that honours difference and gives space to particular needs. The struggle of the bread community is to hold on to this process as it pushes and stretches us in every direction. It is not only in the dough that we can get into a sticky mess. Yet it is out of this nuance and contradiction that the wonder of the community emerges. When a survivor of abuse who declares she hates all men for a moment realises that she trusts Andrew, or when a homeless guy who has nothing of his own has a gift of a loaf for someone else, then these are moments of life-giving connection. This is not an equality of sameness. It is an equality of difference where the depth and contradiction of every individual is respected and held.

So, in putting people at the heart of the bread-making process we are discovering a connection within our disconnection. That is, when we begin to engage with each other around the same table, acknowledging that the only thing that we hold in common is our deep humanity, then a new discourse begins to unfold. This is a discourse that connects us in a lively way in relationship with each other. There are deep levels of mutuality which transcend any neat labels or categories, a fresh way of being within our differences which gives this community both elasticity and form. It grows, it gets knocked back, it is shaped and collapses, it is living and it gives life.

This is only possible if we are serious about claiming all experience as valid. Most of us are not experts when it comes to bread. We begin our encounter from the same place. Arriving at the bread table on any given Tuesday or Thursday will be an unknown selection of people. We never quite know who is going to turn up and we are never the same group twice. Washing hands and finding a place at the table everyone is helped to get going with their bowl of ingredients. Usually it is the person next to you who shows you what to do. Often people apologise, 'I've never done this before.' 'I am rubbish at cookery.' Gradually they realise that this is not a competition. Everyone is in the same situation. It is OK not to be in control. The experience of bread-making shows us that we are not to be judged on some final perfect product. The process is the key. The point of this experience, of any experience, is that we claim it.

The starting point of understanding experience is to 'experience our experience' and to 'experience our experience without fear'. What I mean by this is the need to give ourselves space to listen to and honour the things that have happened to us so that we do not just have experiences but we pause and wonder at the things that are happening to us. Partly it is about living every moment to the full, but more than this it is the desire to reflect upon what life is giving us. Experience is not just a sequence of random occurrences: they form who we are. They are a significant part of what makes us unique. This may prove really difficult and that is why we avoid thinking about them. We may not consider our experience to be of any value, we may be too preoccupied with other things to give this process attention. Experience is not always creative, it can be painful and damaging. Sometimes we choose to forget rather than try to understand what has happened to us. One of the gifts of the bread is that it gives an experience simple enough for anyone to engage with. Believe me, anyone can make bread (with the possible exception of experts!). Because this experience is possible it gives a point of embarkation to the exploration of our other experiences. The bread-making happens in the context of mutual support amid diversity. We begin to see other people within their own story. We begin to see ourselves within our own story.

This is a simple yet strangely radical starting point for a community of faith. There is authenticity within this eclectic gathering. If you make bread here you belong as much as any other bread-maker around the table. If you are here then you belong. The church is whoever is present here today. Tomorrow it will be a different group and so a different church.

In this way we see the imprint of the Gospel on this gathering. I am going to explore with you what that imprint is like, but not yet. First, I want to emphasise the crucial starting point of beginning with experience because I think the inherited church tends to jump too quickly into discussions around authority and orthodoxy. When it does so it becomes the means by which many are silenced. A diverse community such as the one gathering around this bread table will not conform to the expectations of a uniform church. It cannot. Diversity is squeezed out of the churches because people feel afraid to live out of their own questions. Living our experience, claiming its discordance, its struggle, its nonsense is not only the starting point for making bread, it is the starting point for claiming our lives. When we 'experience our experience' we are on a journey of discomfort that may or may not be a journey of faith. This is a risk. There is a risk for the churches around power if the people who come to them retain their choice as to whether to believe or not. There is a risk for individuals around finding their own identity.

Claiming our experience can be the first step to breaking free from other people's construction of reality. If I have the space to tell you my story then I am in the process of claiming who I am. What has happened to me begins to live for me. I can claim it, not as something that is past and finished but as something that continues to shape who I am today. My story is as valid as anyone's story. I may not have done anything particularly spectacular with my life. I may have been abused physically or sexually. I may be sleeping in a bush at the moment because my so-called mate stole my possessions. I may be a highly paid professional in the city. I may be a child. Whoever I am my story is as important as your story. My experience is my experience. This is the starting point of who I am.

If we claim the validity of our own experience we are able to enter into a new way of relating. We can begin to recognise our humanity and in the process we also recognise the humanity of the person standing next to us. As we share the bread, as we tell our stories, as we begin to see that we are valuable, we are able to respect our own lives. It is possible to speak when we know it is possible to be heard without being criticised.

The discovery of this new relational way of being is a surprise to many. Most human encounter is on a surface level. Most days we encounter ourselves and others on a superficial level. Our experiences come and go without much thought. Life on the whole can be an undigested meal. But bread-making is a process. It takes time. There is a rhythm to it that sets the morning aside. You will have to give attention to this experience because it cannot be rushed. Bread rises at its own speed. That depends on the temperature of the room and the excitability of the bakers. Once we had such lively bakers that there was dough flowing over the sides of the bowls faster than we could bake it. Usually bread-making takes a couple of hours with spells of fervent activity punctuated with waiting times while the dough rises. So, inherent in learning to make bread is an understanding of process. There is a pace to bread and to life and to faith, it can neither be rushed nor ignored

Often the church looks for new *models* for Christian communities. I prefer to talk about church as *process*. More importantly faith comes when we begin to give time and space to our experience in the company of other people or on our own. This time and space is the context for us to give attention to what is happening. We become people who learn to find pace and rhythm in our lives. There is the possibility to breathe, to wonder, to converse and to struggle. To be attentive to our experience is not complicated but we need to want to do it. The bread-makers want to do it. They not only take time to sit and talk over coffee but most will also take the opportunity to move to the quiet room to hear the Bible read and to claim some silence. They want to light candles and remember people. They want to say their prayers.

This strikes me as curious. We only ever invite people to 'come and make bread' but more often than not they end up talking about the very deepest parts of their lives. We have an increasing desire to pray. There is now a faith development group once a week and there is an ever-increasing demand for worship. Why is it that this simple bread-making activity inspires people to touch base with their souls? I sense the answer lies somewhere in the interaction between experience, storytelling, remembering and silence. As the discourse and symbols of our everyday lives are cracked open, as we give time and attention to an alternative way of being, then some space begins to open up. Through these cracks emerges a new confidence to speak or to let the silences soak into our being. The more we make bread, the busier we get, the more our community grows, the more it asks for silence.

At lunchtime the bread-makers are joined by one or two people who have jobs in the city and drop by for some quiet in their working day. The smell of bread follows us into the quiet room. We are covered in flour and tired from the kneading. We have shared some important things and struggled alongside people who initially were strangers to us. The Gospel is read. It stands alongside all this experience. We let it stand. We give space for the Gospel and the experience and the silence to converse. Maybe we choose to share something. No one comments or interrupts. When the time is right we light candles to remember those things that are on our minds. We say the Lord's Prayer. We return to the bread table.

This is the simplest of occasions. There may be a few stones or a bowl of water as a focus for our reflection. There are no written words, there are no set patterns, you can come if you want to, leave if you want to. Yet in this context I have heard some of the most remarkable prayers, been astonished by the insights people bring with them, been delighted by the transformation that happens when we give each other time and space and attention. When we are prepared to relate to each other in a new way, equals in our humanity, claiming our own stories, listening other people into their own stories, we discover the gift of the bread. It is with time and space and attention that the human spirit is able to manoeuvre itself to a place of creativity. This may also be a frightening place. Other things may bubble up too. Memories can be sharp. Regrets can be bitter. Grief can be raw. We are learning not to be fearful of these things but to let them also be part of the process. We need to learn to trust the process.

At the bread table the lunch is ready. There is homemade soup, fruit and fresh bread from the oven. Sometimes cheese or doughnuts or one of Carole's famous chocolate and beetroot cakes – Carole is a retired social worker, mum and granny. She has brought up three children and seems always miraculously to appear with cake when we are at our hungriest. We eat, we appreciate the bread, the cake, the company. Many of the homeless guys live a chaotic lifestyle where it is unusual to sit and eat slowly and in company. That is true for others who rush from one thing to another and grab a sandwich in passing. Sitting, eating with wholesome food and conversation is basic to our humanity. It is a point of connection between our bodies and our minds. It is important for our emotional health. Eating is a social activity. We learn to interact with each other around this table. The bread tastes unbelievably good. It has cost us effort to make and we are justifiably proud of it. It is made with organic flour and other natural ingredients. It tastes fabulous and fills us up. So as we delight in our own creativity, in our connection with the earth and with the things that nourish us, we are growing in thankfulness for the simplest things that are so full of wonder.

Growing in gratitude and grace are hallmarks of a community of faith. They are not ethereal qualities. We may simply be grateful for a really good lunch. We may also find a deeper gratitude that comes to us gently, a sense that the bread-making process has helped us take time out for ourselves. That we have unwrapped a little of our own life stories and been able to begin to see them with new eyes. We may be grateful for an encounter, a new friendship, the honour of being able to listen to someone else's story or to help them knead the dough. We may have been surprised by our own laughter or our own tears. Along with eating a lot our community is also known for its deep laughter. There is a great deal of delight in bread-making. We can be surprised by our own ability to create a product that is so good. For some it is the first time that they have ever made something to be admired. Even after five years I am still very proud of my own loaves.

I am also proud of this extraordinary community who will engage so readily with the process of making bread. As each person leaves with their loaves there is a sense in which we have really encountered each other. There is an experience of grace at the heart of this which will now be transported to the recipients of the bread. Who will receive bread? We believe bread is a gift to us so we simply give it away. Everyone chooses where their bread will go. I do not always know exactly where it is heading. It has been sent as a sign of solidarity to various people who are struggling or working in difficult situations. We have a weekend dedicated to survivors of abuse coming up so a few loaves will go in the freezer until Saturday. I know that Carole sometimes gives one to the car park attendant, a loaf goes to a lady in the cutlery department of Lewis's, I often give it away on the train going home and we once posted one to the Archbishop of Canterbury! If God's grace is about gift then it is not for us to know where the gift goes. Gifts are mysteries.

Now the bread-makers have gone I am alone again. I too am learning to 'experience my own experience'. There has been a lot to the last five years. Appointed to Liverpool city centre as a minister without a church or a congregation I have had to believe that this bread-making would make a church become visible. I can see it now, but for a year I wandered around quite lost, walking the streets, talking with people, believing some-how God was ahead of me. Slowly and wonderfully this bread-making community has emerged. Sometimes I wonder where they have all come from. There is something about bread-making that brings engagement from all kinds of inter-esting people. It has also been a process of profound loneliness and lost-ness. I believe now that this is also one of the gifts of bread. In my relationships with the bread-makers I am also learning how to be alone.

As I work with some of the many questions this place provokes in me I am reminded of the stories of another gospel community. Holding the pictures and images of St John's gospel alongside the stories and struggles of this little commu-nity is not an attempt to fit one story inside another story but simply give some room for a conversation between an ancient text and a modern context. This process helps me feel con-nected. It gives me hope in a bigger picture even though I perceive only a fraction; it helps me work with my doubts and struggles, to live my questions and be assured that all is not yet lost. I cannot give an answer to why Jesus said 'I am the door, the light, the vine, the way, truth and life, the resurrection, the bread', but what I can do is let those images rest with us here and listen out for echoes and insights. I want to be real about the dilemma of faith and some of the sharp issues that present themselves to us here and now. In this exploration I am not looking for a neat set of conclusions but rather a way into my own questions.

So, the bread-making community is beginning to open up a new relational way of being which gives time and space and attention to personal story and experience. There is a discovery here of the delight of diversity and its huge challenges. Yes, but how does this experience begin to make a difference in the life of this vast city? There are so many struggling people and this community is both small and vulnerable. How is it possible to understand that the poor are always with us but yet go on believing that the Gospel can make a difference? These are questions for another day; today it is just left for me to wonder where I will take my loaves.

2
Kneading

Clutching two steaming loaves of bread I set off down the four flights of stairs to the street. In the porch Michael is drinking a mug of tea brought out to him by the women from the bookshop. He has the frantic look of a man coming down. His hands are unsteady around the mug. His *Big Issue* badge swings from his pocket with a picture of someone who bears no resemblance to the young man in front of me. Our doorstep is Michael's home at the moment. It is hard for me to describe Michael because the familiar clues to identity are blurred. He is probably in his mid twenties although he could be forty by his appearance, his eyes are brown I think but they do not rest still for long enough to discern a colour, his hair is hidden by a baseball cap. He has designer labels on his tracksuit but it is three sizes too large for him although his shoes are new. His accent is from somewhere in the Midlands and he tells me he used to work as a mechanic. His nails are bitten and his hands shake as he holds his magazines, there are deep yellow stains on the fingers and thumb of his right hand. He smells smoky and damp.

'More bread?' he asks blowing the steam from his tea, avoiding my eyes, shifting from one foot to the other. 'Sure, any good to you today?' 'Not really,' he says, 'have you got any change?' 'Sorry, mate,' I say, 'but I'll bring you something to eat just now.'

Of course I have got change. There are always a few coins in my pocket. I could go to the cash machine and get some. I could nip back upstairs and borrow some money from the office. The offer of food is genuine but unlikely to be realised. I know Michael will be elsewhere by the time I return. He will be off to find some desperate way of getting the next fix.

I do not care what you say, no one chooses this. While the city over-indulges itself on its offer of choices, from the range of coffee in Starbucks to the array of holidays in the travel agent's, Michael just finds the street safer than home. Poor mental health, troubled relationships, abuse or addiction remove choices. Living on a doorstep is never really a choice, it is just marginally better than the rest. If I am to 'experience my experience' it means I am called to experience what it means to be myself in the company of Michael. It is not down to me to rescue, fix or remedy or even to stand alongside because all of these options give me the power. What Michael and I are learning is to see each other and to meet in a genuine encounter. Slowly we are getting to know each other. Imperceptibly this is changing both of us.

As I experience the experience of getting to know Michael and explore what it is to be part of a Christian community in this city I realise that much of what I have inherited as the Gospel is shot through with middle-class assumptions of power. If I applied myself I could probably locate a hostel space, give Michael a good meal, find him some decent clothes, even some chance of rehab. But that is not the point. The point of encounter only comes when I see I cannot change Michael; I must come to value Michael as Michael, and he needs to see the real me with all my struggle and uncertainty too. Then we will change each other. It takes time.

Three political 'hot potatoes' sit on our doorstep. They attract millions of pounds of funding from local, national and European sources. They can make governments squirm or founder. Their assumed names are 'education', 'unemployment' and 'social exclusion', their real name is Michael. There is a whole bureaucracy built around these issues, innumerable

staff employed to administer funding, and a lot of exasperation at the seemingly endless supply of people unable to take
the first step. As if it is a choice they could make.

In St John's gospel we read how Mary takes her costly ointment and anoints Jesus, wiping away the perfume with her
hair. 'Couldn't this have been sold and the money given to the
poor?' Judas challenges. He has a point. Surely practical solutions are a better use of resources. Waste and empty gestures
get us nowhere. 'You will always have the poor among you
but you will not always have me,' replies Jesus. Indeed the
poor are always with us, in the bus station, in the bombed-out
church, sleeping in the multi-storey car park. I have learned
that one of the best places for rough sleepers to spend the
night is a council wheelie bin where it is possible to be dry and
out of sight. The poor are always with us. Not just around, in
the background, to be ignored or pitied, but with us, among
us, part of our society, part of who we are, on our doorstep.
Mary did not give her ointment to 'the poor', some anonymous group of humanity that hung around on the margins.
She gave her ointment to Jesus, poured it out on him, wiped it
with her own hair, took the extravagant risk of ridicule,
because she desired the encounter with someone she was
growing to love. It cost her. The Gospel is teaching me that
transformation rarely happens through agendas and bureaucracy. Transformation happens through encounter.

We encounter people when we are able to meet on equal
terms in our common humanity. When we see and are seen.
Around the large round table at the centre of our bread-
making community we try to live this process. There is always
a different group of people. We have varying levels of affinity
to each other. We hold fears and secrets. As we mix, we
remember and as we remember we tell stories. In the unravel-
ling of these stories we show each other corners of who we are.
Not the whole of ourselves, just hints and memories.

As the successful City of Culture bid causes local politicians
to argue about those who beg on the streets, while national

government looks for new strategies on policing, while Michael survives between pushing and being pushed, we make bread. While religious communities labour to find their way, while churches contract and exist painfully without clergy or resources, while we struggle to deliver statistics that prove growth, this emerging church draws breath through remembering and telling stories. While the political agenda rages outside the door and politicians fearing civil unrest make plans for arrest, Jesus sits at the dinner table with Lazarus, Mary and Martha and with Judas. The poor are always with you, but I am here now, not an issue, not a trouble, not a statistic, but your friend, sitting with you at this table. Don't save everything for the end, don't listen to your own double standards, we will live this moment in the intensity of this encounter, you, me, our story, this will change everything. This is life.

And we argue. We jostle for space, for attention, for praise. We want to be honoured, to be left alone, to be laughed with, to be special. We are defensive, we are possessive, we want to be inventive, we want to make the best bread, we do not want to mess up. Some will have a good time cooking, some will tell their life story, some will wonder if this is really church, some are anxious about the cost of it all, some will spend the morning washing up and some will sit back and wonder what it all means. Lazarus did not say much for someone who had his life returned to him, Mary was away on some leap of imagination, Martha was keeping the show on the road, Judas had an eye to the critics. By the end of the day they were all different. By the end of the day we will all be different. We have seen and been seen. We have encountered each other. We have been held.

As I wander down Bold Street with Michael, thinking about Michael I am aware that Tony is on the next pitch chatting up the passing trade. Tony is an exuberant Glaswegian who often comes to make bread and share the colourful events of his day-to-day life. 'Hello darl,' he accosts a passing student, 'want a *Big Issue* today?' He catches sight of me out of the corner of his eye and waves. At the station entrance is Billy who wants to tell me about his baby, now toddling, and at the bandstand is John, quiet, sullen, with an ulcerated leg and those same restless eyes I have seen so many times at street corners. I give John a loaf and he is pleased. I cannot give quality time and attention to all these people. Maybe I can only honour one person each day. Indeed the poor are always with me but today Michael is on my mind. He is on my mind because he is challenging me about what it means to be an authentic Christian here. Michael can see right through me. He knows I lie to him when I say I have no money. He knows I know about his addiction. Seeing and being seen is not easy. It challenges me to the very heart of my self-perception. It brings me to the centre of my own struggle. If I ask who you are it makes me ask myself who I am.

The intensity of such relatedness needs space. It cannot be creative if it is intrusive. We need to wait for each other. What comes to light is probably not held in the words we exchange but in the cracks in between the words, in the distance between us. I will never understand what it is to be Michael just as he is totally bemused by this strange, wandering vicar-woman who offers him bread. I must un-learn some of my inherited assumptions about the homeless while he un-learns what he has come to expect from church. Why on earth should he bother about the church anyway? Why on earth should I bother about Michael? Yet curiously our lives are mixed up together. It is not just that he lives on my doorstep. It is because I miss him when he is not around. As I put the key in the lock in the morning he is pleased to see me. When visitors call and I do not answer the bell he lets them know when I went out. When I get back he describes to me who it is I have missed. In an odd way we depend on each other. We are becoming friends.

Encounter, then, is about difference and mutuality. It is about allowing someone to be who they are in such a way that it questions who we are ourselves. It has to be authentic because otherwise we are rightly exposed as frauds. (He did not say this because he was concerned about the poor but because he was a thief.) It is about being committed to the silence that lies between us, to the exasperation of not being able to sort things out – to standing with each other in the not understanding. This is how we feel when we begin to live out of our own questions.

This, I sense, is not only the key to being authentic people of faith but also the key to unlocking the door on education, unemployment and social exclusion. This is a big claim that can only happen in small ways. So it is labour intensive and time consuming. How will anyone begin to claim the opportunities that are presented to them if they believe they are invisible or worthless or have no honour? How can we be ourselves if we have never been seen or valued as ourselves? It seems so obvious that we have tended to overlook it – the transforming possibility of genuine, authentic, reciprocated encounter. We know it in our bones. We all know the good teachers were the ones that took a personal interest in us at school and that the best employers are those that value their staff not as units of utility but as human people with gifts and dilemmas. But it is difficult to live it. Partly it is difficult because we are expected to achieve results. How many people has your educational programme enrolled? How many qualifications did the group achieve? What were the learning outcomes? It is right that these questions are asked. God alone knows enough funding is wasted on nonsense schemes that squander time and resources. What about qualitative outcomes? What about those things which make minute, imperceptible differences, those that take time to mature, which are about growing in confidence and self- esteem? How do we measure what was fun or gave us most satisfaction?

When Billy first came to make bread he did not speak. He insisted on wearing his cap down over his eyes. He was suspicious, sullen and left before the end. Two years on he is still selling the *Big Issue* but he greets me across the street. He is now allowed to pick his kids up from school and sometimes they stay for the weekend. He took them across to the Sea Life Centre in Seacombe the other day on the Mersey ferry and they had fish and chips. It is not a 'quantitative, measurable outcome'. It is about Billy and a bit of leaven in the lump of Billy's life. It does not give me any very credible statistical returns, Billy and his kids. I really do not see him that often and he does not come to Sunday worship. But hey, it is good news.

When we mix the bread ingredients in a bowl there is a point at which they turn into a gloopy, sloppy mess. It is at this point we have to put the mixing spoon down and get our hands into it. At this moment 'kneading the bread' is more of a romantic perception than a reality. It squishes between your fingers, the bowl slides all over the table, there is dry flour at the bottom and a slimy concoction sticking your fingers together. You have to believe it is going to be something. Sometimes it is hard to believe. Someone may need to hold the bowl still for you or encourage you not to give up. It takes time, making bread. It takes belief in the bread-ness of bread. There is something holy about standing with each other in this process, in the not understanding of our lives, in the nonsense of who we are, in believing that something will emerge from all this mess. Jesus sat at the table with his friends, with a fusspot and a dreamer, with a cheat and a dead man who had no words. He said to the person who rubbished the giver of ointment 'leave her alone'. He wanted to honour Mary's illogical, senseless gesture because he saw to the heart of what Mary was becoming. He wanted to receive the gift – not because Mary was being good but because she was being Mary. For Mary, Jesus was the only person in the room, for Jesus there was both a group of mixed-up individuals each of whom was perceived, yet also, at that moment, there was only Mary. They saw each other. They saw death, life, the moment, the significance, the priestliness, the intensity, the drama, the sorrow, the longing, the transformation. They connected into each other's soul and the ointment was the means of saying it all. Let her be. This is holiness.

Church did not teach me this. Michael, Billy, Tony and the other bread-makers are teaching me this. Church taught me I had to be good. When I was a child I was taught that if I was really good Jesus might want me for a sunbeam – and if not exactly a sunbeam at least I got to go to the seaside with the Sunday School. Church has taught me a whole set of values – about sexuality and how I am to be a responsible steward of my time and money and what it means to be married. Church schools me to believe that there are a set of ideals to which I should aspire. Church has taught me to keep my own counsel because I might inadvertently (or deliberately!) be a heretic. I have been taught to be good. Now I must learn to be real. I am finding it hard to be real because I have spent a lot of my life trying not to be real. Being good has encouraged me to conform to a set of assumed values. Because I am reasonably adept at living within these parameters they feel quite comfortable. I have a good enough education to enable me to wriggle out of many awkward corners. I have a family that tries to love me, and food in the cupboard. I can drive and read and understand (most) jokes. I am integrated into polite company, I have money in the bank, at least for a week after pay day. Being real is a nuisance. It means I have to see Michael.

Remember the story of Pinocchio the wooden puppet who lied to the puppeteer and whose nose grew longer and longer? How the old man who had made him set him free? How he set off on his travels and got taken in by all kinds of cheats and liars and finally swallowed by a whale? And only when he had made a complete mess of it all and he had broken Geppetto's heart did Pinocchio lose his strings and become real. Only then did the puppet-maker who had chiselled him out of a piece of wood become his father. And do you remember Jonah who had a similar big-fish experience and ended up vomited onto a beach? Jonah was furious with God because he had not become the hero he wanted to be. He sat under a plant and sulked all day. The plant made him feel safe until the sun withered it and then he had to understand that God's ways were bigger and deeper and more loving, more perplexing than any of his straight-line thinking. Do you remember the story in the gospels where a crowd gathers to listen to Jesus and the disciples panicked because there was no food and everyone was getting hungry? Somehow from nowhere five loaves and two fishes appeared that not only fed the crowd but also filled the empty baskets that someone had strangely brought to the event? Transformations. There are a lot of connections between loaves and fishes.

Learning to live without strings is different from living without rules. Holiness does not call us into a life of destruction or licentiousness. On the contrary it is an invitation into living a connection between all that the Scriptures teach us, the life and tradition of our faith, the wisdom of other people and our own day-to-day experience. This will take all our intelligence, wit and integrity. It is not so much about discovering a neat set of answers to life, the universe and everything, but more an authentic engagement with our own questions. It is about prayer, the discovery of the wonder and nuance and contradiction of the world around us and a head-on experience with pain. No wonder the church is often too frightened to go there.

Jesus was in deep trouble. Outside the door the authorities were looking for ways to kill him, there was a traitor at the dinner table. It is not politically shrewd to give a voice to the poor, it is not economically sound to feed a whole crowd with a few donated loaves and fishes, it is not socially acceptable to eat with the scapegoats. He was on his way to crucifixion. That was why Mary anointed him. Because dying and being a king were part of the same story.

I have wondered if holiness is about being whole. Being good is often about trying to be more, being complete, aiming to achieve some educational or celestial target. We are products of the twentieth and twenty-first centuries. We have a post-Enlightenment view on progress which has its sights on some bigger and more complete world view. In ministerial self-appraisal we are encouraged to review the way we work and ask if there are any areas in which we sense we are not competent. Why? Is it so we can plug the gaps and become more rounded practitioners? Or is it so that we can say 'I'm rubbish at that' and find someone else for whom it is easy? We often laugh at job descriptions for clergy for which Mother Teresa would not be shortlisted. Why do we equate holiness with being omnicompetent? Holiness cannot be about being complete because none of us will ever be complete, we are all fragile, broken, struggling human beings whose gifts are limited by ability, culture and opportunity. There is, I suspect, an element of wholeness about it – not as a prescription for individualism but as a way we come to value each other. Between us we have the possibility of becoming more whole than on our own. Faith is about working that out together, not just for ourselves or indeed for the church but for society, for Michael.

Michael is homeless because of socio-economic factors that have squeezed him to the threshold. He is homeless because key networks of family cohesiveness have disintegrated. He is homeless because other parts of society have claimed their rights with louder voices than he has. He is homeless because the politics of this country view drug abuse as a criminal rather than a medical condition. He is homeless because of me and people like me who have assumed the centre ground and pushed him to the edge. We are implicit in this. I have bread, Michael wants cash, I will not give him cash because I make a moral judgement about how he will use it and what is good for him, he disappears. Michael and I need to learn how to see each other.

Maybe also there is something about holiness that joins us up. That encourages us to see each other as whole – as body, mind and spirit. I am learning that making bread crosses these false divisions. It is both wholesome and nutritious, physically demanding and emotionally rewarding and in this way opens up an understanding of Eucharist that is about the whole of us being connected, mysteriously, to God's intention through Jesus for the whole of creation. It is also contradictory. It is not the sort of wholeness that gets everything wrapped up. A lot of life is just a mess and anyone who says that having faith will resolve all problems is deluded. Maybe we are just called to hold the bowl for people while we work it out together, while we go on pummelling the nonsense. That is what Mary was doing. She was saying 'I believe you are the anointed king', while the crowd gathered outside and execution was imminent. It did not stop it happening of course. Despite the triumphal entry into Jerusalem the following day, Judas still betrayed Jesus, the disciples fled, and the Lord of heaven was crucified between a couple of house-breakers. That does not mean Mary was wrong, it means Mary was real. She could see that there was something going on that was bigger than the events that were unfurling. She could perceive that being holy was more than surviving – it was about a connection with a different story. Jonah got there in the end too, despite his sulk, and the disciples grasped it eventually after Pentecost. God's story is about transformation. It is about experiencing our own experience in the light of God's encounter with us. Mary, who had been so annoyed with Jesus for being late when Lazarus was dying – 'If only you had been here my brother would not have died' – suddenly saw the breaking in of a different story. She began to live life in the light of death.

So, maybe holiness is about wholeness, but it is also about holding. Now, 'holding' is a difficult word because it might be construed as 'grasping'. Jesus said to Mary in the garden, 'Do not cling to me'. Jesus needed to be free. He was not to be owned by Mary. His appearance was to enable her to go on believing and to carry the news of resurrection to the rest of the disciples. I cannot stop Michael disappearing. This community is not a cult that will not allow people to leave. We must be semi-permeable to the culture in which we are immersed – people come and go as if by osmosis. That is healthy. But there is something about holding that implies solidarity among friends. Standing alongside each other in our muddles and mess is part of the way of faith. It is not about problem-solving, or knowing better, or keeping a lot of sacred answers. It is about love. Remember the story of the father who let his son go off with half the family inheritance? How that father waited and watched the horizon, longing for the return of what has come to be known as 'the prodigal son' but might more aptly be entitled 'the typical son'? How, when the son returned there were no recriminations or blame lobbed in the direction of the boy, just a celebration, a thanksgiving that he was home? Who waits and watches for Michael? Last week a vendor overdosed and there was no one at the funeral except the undertaker. It was a pauper's funeral in a communal grave because there was no money to pay for anything else. Who sees, who waits, who scans the horizon?

Holding is not just about physical holding, although it may be appropriate sometimes for this to be so, it is also about remembering, holding in the mind's eye, recognising the common humanity of those around us. This is hard. There are so many people who challenge us to the point of despair. Why is it that some people never manage to get a job and keep it? Why do others drift in and out of prison? What about the pimps and drug-dealers? What about the money-lenders who trap people in impossible cycles of debt? The poor are always with us because the corrupt are always with us. Jesus prayed in his despair, 'My God, my God, why have you forsaken me?' Sometimes there is no limit to the scheming and depravity of the powerful, the fearful and the insane. Judas was the keeper of the money bag and used to help himself to what was put in it. Judas sat at the table along with Mary and Martha and Lazarus and Jesus. We live always in the company of people who will betray us, who will destroy us, who will manipulate us to their own self-seeking ends. Despite this we are called to uphold each other, to go on believing that bread will be bread and that it is possible for people to discover their lives.

Is this not a calling to the church? We have the skills. But it might cost us everything, watching and waiting, longing and paying attention, hoping and nagging, seeing the divine image in each other. I think it could be possible, if we stopped worrying about our own survival and started to recognise what is going on around us. It is costly though, this holding thing. It means hanging on in there when everyone else has made off. People who are trying to survive have learned to lie and manoeuvre. We must be canny about that. We cannot, single-handedly go around rescuing the whole world. We can only see who we see and hold fast to 'that which is good'. It is about a new way of being with each other that is not being led by any particular agenda. It is about trusting that possibly, if we go on believing in people, even in our mess and muddle, then something surprising could emerge.

If we are to be real we need to let go of a lot of things that inspire us to seem good. This is hard when the church has set parameters on behaviour and lifestyle that are often unreal. The bread-making community is comprised mostly of people who have fallen out from or fallen out with the church. Yet they are people of surprising faith. When a gay person has experienced a church community praying for them to be 'healed' of their homosexuality or a lone parent has had the church prayer group praying for her to get back together with her abusive husband then there is justifiable anger. We do not like living with blurred edges, yet life is like this. I am coming to realise that being gay is as natural to a gay person as being heterosexual is natural to me. And that sometimes marriage is best relinquished for something better. It is no good sitting under an ecclesiastical bush and sulking that the foliage does shade us from the scorching sun. We have to get to grips with a different relationship with God and a different understanding of ourselves. Ways of living in the light of the sun. Being real is about cutting the strings that have a puppeteer-creator manipulating who we are in some predetermined staging of life. Pinocchio had to go and live his own story, so did Jonah, so do we. We will undoubtedly get in a mess and take all kinds of wrong turns. We cannot always get it right, we cannot always be good but we need to be known by our intention to be authentic to the Gospel. Go on believing in the Father who scans the horizon for us, and the Son who was both anointed and betrayed at the same party.

Maybe the church is called to live its life in the light of death. We are at the point of seeing the death of our inherited faith communities. The threshold between the worshipping Sunday congregations and the ordinary people of the city is often too high to breach. We cannot expect any kind of revival that brings people into church on our terms. Church could do with sitting on the threshold and see who is there waiting for them to return.

The evening is beginning to draw the colours from the sky. The city is changing shifts. The shops have closed and the shutters are being pulled across the windows. There is a statue of an embracing couple on Bold Street. It is by the local sculptor Steve Broadbent and entitled 'Reconciliation'. It is a larger version of a small bronze he made for a friend when they had fallen out. There are replicas of this statue in Belfast and Glasgow – two other formerly sectarian cities. We have learned so much, yet we have so much to learn. So much to learn about reconciliation and our own part in the process. How when we experience our own experience we are called into a new reality, a deep honesty and the living out of these questions. The poor are always with us, and so are the issues around poverty, but they are not just 'issues', these economic and personal dilemmas have faces and names. They are our companions and they will change us. With Michael I am brought to confront my own questions about responsibility, my own implication in poverty, the desire to make all things new. How is it possible for this community to be a countersign, willing to look for safe spaces for genuine encounter? There is so much I could be called into being and doing, yet I am only one person and after talking with John I am tired. The poor may be always with us but when I get back to our door-way there is no sign of Michael. His sleeping bag is tucked in a bin bag and wedged behind the drainpipe. I am going to take this second loaf home with me tonight. It is time I saw my children too.

3
Shaping

When I get back in the morning Michael is lying right across the threshold. He is not sleeping but deep down in his bag, huddled against the cold. I step over him and go inside. We have set loaves aside for today and they need to be warmed. Col is concerned. Today we offer safe space for survivors of abuse. It does not feel safe if you have to step over a man to reach the door. The poor are always with us and today we are wishing they would go away so that we can open up a different kind of space. We make soup and begin to think of a strategy for the doorway.

We are living with a lot of questions about safety. Is there a relationship between safety and salvation? In the city we make each other vulnerable by trying to share the same place. Maybe safety is an illusion and that means salvation is an illusion. Is there anything to be said in the face of abuse and the effects of abuse? How will Col and I offer safe space today?

Col says, 'Of course this is not safe space. Nowhere is completely safe. All we can offer is a safer place, a breathing space, somewhere to let down our guard for a while.' Ironically, when we do this we all become less safe. Contact with people who have been abused has been something that has just come to this community, something which took me by surprise. It was in the course of a seemingly ordinary conversation that someone first disclosed abuse. When it happens you are given the choice to listen or not to listen; I have made the choice to try to listen. Since then I have encountered a whole network of survivors and we have seen this contact to be a gift to our community. We are, after all, a church that is freer than most to engage where the wind blows. There have been times though when these encounters have seemed anything but a gift. I have listened to some stories that have rattled me, got into my head, made me furious, shocked me beyond any rational response. Rape by fathers, by brothers or priests. Violations by women as well as to women. Secret rituals, in churches, in graveyards, sacrifices of animals and babies. Police corruption, inept doctors, theft of medical records, abuse carried out in the name of religion: 'Sleep with me and God will heal your past abuse. I will make you clean again.' Stories of what abusers have done would make you sick. And it is always harder to tell than to hear.

Many of the gospel images are unhelpful for survivors. Like the vision of a sheepfold with a man lying across the door which is given to us by the author of St John's gospel. Jesus offers this as a vision of security for believers. What worse scenario could there be for survivors of abuse than being herded into a pen with no way out? That is not safety. That is being trapped in some nightmare of vulnerability. Abuse is not just about what happened to us in the past, it permeates the whole of what happens next. It is the robbery of childhood, and that can never be returned. Robbery is theft with violence. Abuse is not about sex, it is about power. Wherever there are images of power, they will trigger memories of abuse for survivors. What has happened to us and what memories that holds is intimately linked with the way we come to faith. Gospel images have tended to be interpreted by the powerful.

Before I went to university I was a shepherd for a while. I spent a year 'watching flocks by night' and learning the complications of heads and limbs that present themselves when lambs are born. Among other things I began to know the sheep, that munched and belched their way through the night – the one with the spot, the one with the black triplets, the cantankerous old ewe with a penchant for head-butting, the inexperienced teg that made such a fuss in labour – each revealed their individual characteristics. That is how you got to know them and name them. That is why we have to upgrade our view of sheep. Sheep are not the woolly-back conformists you might believe them to be. They have style.

Jesus knew that so much better than those of us who hold a Postman Pat view of the countryside. He understood that sheep had names and lived with terrors. That is why shepherds went with their sheep onto the dangerous hillsides and lay across the doorway. It was because of the wolves in the night. The Psalmist knew this too when he wrote, 'O Lord my God, I take refuge in you; save and deliver me from all who pursue me; or they will tear me like a lion and rip me to pieces with no one to rescue me' (Psalm 7). If we are to survive we need safer space, while we rest, while we regain our strength, while we confide in people who will believe what we say. Col goes down to the door to greet people and let them in. This is not an inclusive community today – 'I tell you the truth, the man who does not enter the sheep pen by the gate is a thief and a robber' – this is a place where named yet anonymous individuals can be what they want to be without fear of wolves in sheep's clothing. It is hard for gentle, gracious, vulnerable men to appreciate that they too are looked on with suspicion and are not welcome here today. Making safer space is not only about the power we hold but the power we are perceived to hold. Too often the church has been the cause of abuse, or silent in the face of disclosure. A clerical collar can instil deep terror and I have left mine at home.

Gradually people begin to arrive: old ladies with shopping bags, young women with nose rings, smart, scatty, loud, diffident, colourful, drab women all of whom would fill you with wonder if you met them. They would fill you with wonder because they are so ordinary. Some are mums, teachers, professors, ministers, counsellors; they do voluntary work, they arrange flowers, they are artists and poets. I am certain that you will know people who have survived abuse and will have no inkling of their past. Mostly, survivors do not go around proclaiming the hardships they have endured; they get on with living and taking on the wide world. That should not bring us to underestimate the struggle that leads from abuse to flourishing. The struggle that is lived day by day, through flashbacks, memories and physical scars which damage self-confidence and growth. Abuse is a predator that prowls through memories devouring self-esteem. Like any bereavement you do not really get over it, you live with the gap. The gap of a murdered childhood cannot be filled. There will always be bits missing, things that cannot be talked about with those closest to you, confusing, blurred recollections. These might need to be expressed in cathartic ways like self-harm or eating disorders. There will be perfectly rational fears that may appear irrational like being terrified of walking into the middle of a room. Someone is frightened of touching the bread dough. Many survivors need counselling or psychotherapy by skilled practitioners. We do not offer that and we say so. What is really important is that we do not stray into our own incompetence. Setting realistic boundaries is also about safety. It is not healthy to encourage dependency and it gives false signals if we say we are always available. Clear guidelines around appropriate contact are crucial. It does not help any-one, least of all survivors, if we make false promises.

Col has prepared for the weekend with great care. The toilets contain a selection of perfumes, deodorants and cos-metics. The kitchen has non-intrusive volunteers. There is a quiet room with candles and big cushions. There is a corner with toys. Creative arts materials cover the table: clay and felt-tipped pens, glue, glitter. It is a day to use as we choose.

I am having a theological conversation with myself about salvation. How does it relate to safety? This is not an exercise in systematic theology; it is a struggle that has huge ambigui-ties, contradictions and paradoxes. If the Gospel is about salvation then what are we being saved from and what are we being saved for? Being saved 'from' something implies that we are being redeemed from ourselves, from our secret sins, from the things that we can change. This is a view of the world (is it a male view?) in which we are able, with God's help, to reform ourselves. It is a powerful perspective in which we are free to take a different path, claim different values, be forgiven and move on. But yet survivors (mostly women) do not live out of this reality. What has been taken from them is not a result of their sin. It has happened to them and so they are not totally free to make choices. Often they are expected to embark on a journey of faith in which this abuse is ignored or treated as something of the past that it is their duty to forgive and then move forward. Salvation has an intimate link with safety because it is only when we feel safe enough to engage with our history that there is a possibility to see what we have been saved for. To say we are survivors is to proclaim we are not victims. One day we might say we are not survivors either but fulfilled, joyful human beings – that is what we are being saved for.

On the whole our inherited churches appear to be fairly safe places. They are indoors, clean and dry, you can sit reasonably comfortably and still in the middle of a Sunday morning without too much of a challenge. It is possible to follow the whole thing from the book and have a nice cup of tea before you go home. That is fine unless you are claustrophobic, shy, schizophrenic, cannot read, incontinent, an overactive child, or are on a night shift. Then being in church is not at all safe, it is like walking through a minefield in flippers. This is not safety, it is an illusion of safety. One of the biggest criticisms of church is that it is hypocritical, and you can see why. We preach 'salvation' but we do not look like pilgrims who are walking through 'the shadow of the valley of death'. We appear more like people who have had a good breakfast and are waiting for the omnibus edition of *EastEnders*. Now this is not to say that church people do not have issues and problems, it is just that probably church is the last place on earth they would consider sharing them. We are much more likely to seek out the company of special, trustworthy friends and have a good old moan midweek over a cup of coffee.

So safety can in fact be an illusion dressed up as benign indifference. This does not strike me as embodying salvation. In reality we should be thoroughly scared because we are far from safe. We are like the grass in the fields, here today and gone tomorrow, we live our lives in the context of a Western response to terrorism and we are facing environmental meltdown. Survivors live their lives in the context of their death. They have faced annihilation and know they are not safe – at least they are more real about that possibility than those who choose to ignore danger.

Then there are Michael and Col who live out of another context of being unsafe. Michael does not have much impetus to think of the consequences of global warming – truth to tell he could do with the globe being a bit warmer. Michael needs food and company. Col needs a place to be real. We need safety before we can address our vulnerability. We need to know we are vulnerable before we can express a need for safety. We need to feel safer before we can acknowledge that we are unsafe. We need to know we are unsafe before we can search for safety. The people of Israel believed in a Promised Land but they had to traverse a wilderness and a precariously poised tidal wave before they reached it.

What has this got to do with the Kingdom of God? It seems to me that salvation is one of those reverses for which the Gospel is notorious. Those who sense they are safe will suddenly be thrown into a context in which they lose that illusion. Christ does not bring safety to the comfortable but disrupts accepted norms, challenging our assumptions, taking a side swipe at the illusion of security. On the contrary, for the dispossessed and the vulnerable, salvation begins with the safety of physical and emotional space. It is about being warm and dry. For all of us salvation is being seen – about living in the company of the shepherd who joins us on the dangerous hillside. For an abuser to be seen it should bring terror, for an abused person to be seen, when they are really valued for the unique person they are, it should bring honour. So it is not so much about a state of being but about a way of being. Jesus brings us salvation by living in the doorway between safety and annihilation. He puts his body where his faith lies. He does not wipe out the past but gives us the possibility of a new way of relating. Is this the good news of salvation of which the gospels speak? I sense only if we wake in the morning to the shepherd calling us by name onto the wide open hillside. Church is not a self-help group. A sheepfold is not a prison. It should be a place of reconnection with the story of salvation from which we are called out into life in all its fullness.

That is all very well except that for an abused child there has been no protection. God has not slept in the doorway and stopped the abuser appearing in the night. The abused feel repulsed and responsible for something over which they had no control. Where is God in all this? How is it possible to believe that anything or anybody is safe any more? I think this can only become a possibility if we are prepared to acknowledge that we are not able to make the church safe. We cannot eliminate abuse or abusers. There are dark, sinister figures who stalk the hillsides and we do not know where they are. We can, however, demonstrate an intention for safety, a desire for a place where abused people can reclaim their power, can be heard, can be honoured. So we are called to acknowledge our own potential for being places of abuse, to engage with the very best practice to prevent it and be prepared to listen when disclosures are made.

Life in all its fullness is not just the enjoyable and expansive parts but the length and breadth of our relations with each other. Life in all its fullness is about living a different kind of relatedness. If we are to 'experience our experience' then we need to be real about every aspect of that experience, we cannot just choose the palatable parts. As the day progresses there is a thawing of our unease. Some amazing works of art are taking shape and some expressive writing. These emerge from deep-down places. 'Arise oh Lord and deliver me, O my God! Strike my enemies on the jaw; break the teeth of the wicked' (Psalm 3). The paintings are messy, full of red, black and purple. There is an outpouring of anger. Someone rolls hers up and lobs it out the window to laughter mixed with tears. These women are teaching me that it can be creative to engage with this level of pain, to bring anger into the visible world. That it can be held if we do not panic but accept what is brought out into the open. That if we experience this experience together there is living water that can spring up within us.

One of the outcomes of being abused is often there is a struggle to form deep, trusting, long-term relationships. It is better to keep wandering than to be committed. This is understandable, but it leads to a continuing cycle of isolation. If it is difficult to know what are appropriate boundaries, it can be very frightening to get close to anyone. That is why the people with the power need to take full responsibility for setting the limits. Children in non-abusive situations learn how to negotiate friendships as a natural part of their growing up. Where there is abuse there is often isolation from peer groups and a secret double life that means friends will only ever know part of the story. Adult friendships and church relationships need to be overt about the boundaries that are operating. If we are fudging them we need to know we are fudging them. They must always be relationships that have exits. Deep wells of friendships can be drawn from, which can provide a rich source of growth and wonder.

Drawing from these wells brings the possibility of naming things: the naming of experiences, however hard it is to find the words; the naming of the struggle when people who have been abused feel under pressure to forgive those things for which they are not responsible; the naming of the continuing presence of pain which undermines a sense of being whole and healthy; sometimes the naming of abusers. I have travelled quite a journey listening to survivors' stories. We have visited places that hold memories and we have sat together in the pain of remembering. Some parts of stories have been written on scraps of paper as they have poured out in the middle of the night. I have not read all of these but we have shredded them and burned them and made them into paper boats and floated them out to sea. Over Lent we have worked at a huge collage. It was a picture of a child on a see-saw, a playground scene, a place where children should be safe and have fun. Of course it held other memories. The child was on the raised arm of the see-saw, high in the air, her pig-tails flying out behind her. On the heavy end there was noth-ing, at least nothing visible. The weight that kept the child in the air, unable to touch the ground and play elsewhere, was the unspoken, invisible weight of abuse.

The good shepherd is not a hired hand. She is committed to these sheep with all their idiosyncrasies and pain. This is something that takes time and energy. It is not something to be taken lightly. Anyone who assumes this role needs to have proper supervision and learn what is appropriate. I can tell you it will scare you witless. The shepherd is not a stranger and that is the double bind for people who have been abused. Most abuse happens by someone you know, someone you trust, who has authority over you, someone you love. So that means that we who hear the stories must be doubly trust-worthy. We must take responsibility for setting good guide-lines and not become yet another abuser, even by mistake. Transformations come through such encounters, but we need to be very wise.

Think for a moment about the salt in the bread. If you have ever left the salt out of a loaf you will know that the resulting tasteless mass is totally unpalatable. It is like eating a lump of cardboard. If, however, you add too much salt (like the time someone mistook tsp to signify tablespoons) then the resulting loaf will make you sick. Sexual abuse takes our sexuality which is something that can bring delight and fulfilment to our lives and overlays it with the power to destroy. It is a good thing turned bad. It takes a fundamental relationship – a father to a child – and puts too much power into it so that the child is overwhelmed by the very person they should trust the most. So people who have been abused often have some residual love and respect for the perpetrators of their abuse. They may still try to protect them by taking on a mantle of guilt and secrecy. Standing within this tangle is like standing inside a knot, it squeezes the breath out of you.

Survivors have at times been really angry with me. I have tried to engage with their stories with deep intensity but I have also had other things to do. Struck by memories that implicate people in authority, people who have ignored cries for help, I have sometimes been seen to represent that authority. I have been sworn at quite violently, I have had to weather episodes of anger and silence. This is not a head response, this is an emotional response; it is not an adult response, it is a child response. But it is real. It is very hard to hang on in there. At times I have been really scared about what I was getting into. Not least because the abuser has the potential for killing victims if they are found, and no doubt those who are found to be helping them too. We have had to be rigorous about confidentiality and canny about the boundaries we have put in place, especially among our church community. We have had to bring things out into the open while still keeping the lid on them to protect ourselves against unnecessary risk. It has been one of the most creative engagements I have made, but it has been terrifically demanding. We have definitely not done everything right. But it has mattered that we have not given up. We have been ruthlessly honest with each other and I have been fortunate that many of these amazing women have been patient in teaching me and have demonstrated strong, personal, challenging relationships with God.

At lunchtime the bread has been warmed and is on the table with soup and cheese. This is a feast of honour. It is a simple banquet that gives tribute to women who, despite everything, still believe in a God of love. How can this be so? How is it possible to believe in a God of protection when life has brought violation and damage? I cannot tell you the answer to this. All I know is that I sit in the company of women who still desire to pray for integrity and justice. I honour their resilience and faith. Lunch is good and there are some plans for worship this afternoon using the poems and pictures that have emerged. I am a bit perplexed by a mood board on one of the walls that has been the space for some spontaneous graffiti. I am aware that the Bishop of Liverpool is coming for lunch tomorrow and might not be too impressed by what he sees. I share my concern and am told quite firmly what I should do – the board stays! The bread church has a responsibility to give survivors a voice back to the church. We need courage to come out of the closet together. We should not cover up what has happened any more. But it is a hard step to take while still offering a sense of safety. We must own that we all have responsibility for listening attentively to the voices of abused people so that we can act together as agents of transformation for the whole church community.

Jesus said, 'I am the door; anyone who comes into the fold through me will be safe.' The Psalmist says, 'Now in peace I shall lie down and sleep; it is you alone, Lord, who let me live in safety' (Psalm 4:8).

After lunch we plan an away day. We are going to go to Chester to fly kites. We will take a picnic and the bubble-blowing machine and afterwards we will have ice creams by the river.

I think we have made 'salvation' into a burdensome word. When Jesus spoke to Nicodemus, that poor troubled old Pharisee who slipped in to talk things over under cover of darkness, Jesus said he should be 'born again'. He told Nicodemus that he should live out in the daylight, that he should believe, that God loves him, that he will not perish. He says to follow the spirit which blows where it wills. Jesus says it is evil men who slink about in the darkness and hope that they will not be discovered. He says that those who believe – whoever they are and whatever has happened to them – can come out into the bright sunlight in the middle of the day and feel the wind on their faces. Jesus says 'Live'.

Survivors are greatly burdened by other people's sins. They can feel guilty and unclean because of what has been done to them. They often feel responsible for something for which they are not responsible. We have tended to burden them further by talk of their need to forgive their abusers. That somehow they have to be cleansed of the past through their own determination, or worse still that they should try to forget. Jesus says to be born again is to live as children of daylight, to fly kites and blow bubbles and unlock a different childhood in the company of those with whom you can feel safer. When the new lambs come out into the field in the Spring they play, their fussy mothers chomp the grass and call them to order but it does not stop them from frolicking and leaping around, testing their wobbly legs, trying the grass and spitting it out, jumping off the backs of the old ewes as they try to sleep. Salvation is not a threat, it is a promise. When Jesus said 'No one comes to the Father except by me' I am sure that he did not mean this passage to be used as a threat to the half-believer or the non-believer or the adherent to another faith. Too often it has been used to prop up an exclusive view of the Kingdom where the door is shut on anyone who tentatively finds their way to faith. It holds an extra terror for survivors who fear that approaching a father might lead them once again into a place where they lose themselves. I suggest it is a passage that is not intended as an exclusive threat but as a demonstration of a way. This way is about opening doors not closing them. It is a call to discover a new relationship with God as a trustworthy father. Salvation is the gift of this new relationship. I acknowledge that for some survivors the renewing of a parent relationship connected to God is impossible. This reality calls the church into exploring new and more creative images, but whatever language we use I want to affirm that the shepherd calls us because he loves us.

There is a saying that shepherds know: 'Shear your flock in May, shear your flock away.' It implies that taking the shears to the sheep's fleeces before the threat of the last cold snap of winter could lead to their death by pneumonia. It is best to wait until the weather is set fair. Five years on from the beginning of this bread-making project I sense we are becoming 'June people'. There is an increasing independence within this community. We are being called out by name. There seems an intrinsic link between finding a safer place and being able to move out onto the dangerous hillside. The more people believe in us and we are honoured and trusted, the more we will risk. In the daytime, in the summer, the shepherd lets the sheep be free.

Survivors of abuse can transform the church. They are not hapless victims, they are flesh-and-blood gutsy people who have deep rich stories to tell. They can inform us about the use of space – how it can be safer for all of us. They can tell us what is good practice, how we can give each other room to flourish and grow. How we can begin to trust the process of discovering who we are becoming together. They do not need to be wrapped in cotton wool, they need to be heard. June people can shed their coverings. They can be free to dance and laugh and breathe deep fresh summer air. That is how it should be for all of us as we claim our space together as human beings. No one should live perpetually in a closet. The abused person is not responsible for their own abuse. It is hard for all of us to work this through. As we break bread together we know only too well the pain that it symbolises, the pain that Christ has mysteriously shared with all victims through his death, but we also celebrate the transforming possibility of new life that occurs despite all that. Belief in the possibility of new life that comes through the breaking of the vicious circles of death and destruction is the gift to our bread breaking community. We have to believe it can be true. Jesus said, 'I am the good shepherd'; he also said, 'I am the resurrection and the life.'

The church has spent a lot of time and energy on crafting its policy on safeguarding children and vulnerable adults – rightly so. It also needs to give survivors time and attention to begin to show us all how to have life in all its fullness. We are called into open spaces to live life to the full. That is why thresholds are about exits as well as entries. I hope that Michael will not still be on the doorstep when these guys set off for home. They need to wander out into the street and mingle anonymously with the crowd. They will become invisible again and be the people they are called to be in the context in which they live. They need room to grow and flourish, have space to be whoever it is God calls them to be. That is salvation – not a wholly separated state of affairs on the other side of judgement day, but a call into a new way of living. Called by the shepherd who knows our names and calls us to the places where we can be nourished, be real and have fun.

Yes, but we cannot make these things happen overnight. Sometimes we must wait within the silence, in a place beyond words and simply hold the questions and live out of the not-knowing. Live this Saturday somewhere between death and resurrection.

4

Waiting

Sunday morning and the pavements shine wet and grey. The herring gulls teeter on the wet roofs, bills dibbling under their wings, feet splayed for balance. Shutters are closed like lids over the interior secrets of shop windows. The plash of a bicycle swishes a discarded chip paper into a mush at the edge of the one-way street. Sleeping souls in loft apartments pull pillows round their ears with plans for coffee and the newspaper at noon. I am aware of a hole in the sole of my shoe through which my sock draws water like wet blotting paper. I have walked a long way this year.

Once a month this bread community meets for worship on a Sunday morning. The request for worship was a surprise to me and led to a rather funny conversation in which we tried to find time in our diaries for some space. We rejected evenings because we were all tired after work and Saturday is my day off, so then someone hit on the idea of Sunday! What is worship for a community such as this one? How do we engage with silence and talking in creative ways? How are tired people recreated by the experience of worship rather than burdened with a barrage of words and tasks? How do we find a sense of holiness at the core of our lives which are so beset with contradictions? As with many questions for which we do not know the answer this community begins in a different place, with making bread.

Turning the key in the lock I relish the prospect of having

the place to myself for an hour – a rare treat these days. In the beginning it was always this way. Now I welcome some time alone. It is never totally quiet here, there is always the sound of a siren or car radio, but there is at least a chance for some solitude. I take the plastic bowl and spoon from the cupboard, nine spoons of yeast, one of honey, three of salt ... there is a reassuring rhythm to the mixing of dry ingredients, then the addition of warm water, the physical pounding of the dough. The lump becomes elastic, relaxes and starts to claim its own shape.

At eleven o'clock people will begin to drift in for worship. Rubbing sleep from tired eyes, stretching themselves into the day. There is a choice of how to spend the time. In the quiet room, silence is held. The middle room has the Sunday papers and books of poems and novels. In the kitchen, the ingredients for lunch will be claimed and chopped with a chatter of conversation. We can move where we choose, in and out of silence, connecting with our own need, listening to our own voice or the voices of others. It is time to pay attention to ourselves, to be re-created. My need for silence seems to grow daily. It has become a hunger in me. It is not about an absence of speech or noise. It is the desire to clear the decks of my own cluttered interior life. I long to give the contradictions and delights of the experience I am experiencing some room to breathe, space for the longings inside myself to have clearance for manoeuvre.

I am also afraid of silence. I resist it and will find an endless stream of avoidance strategies. Sometimes it is like standing on the edge of a dark abyss with only the terror of the absence of things. Before the beginning there was no word. The rumour of that awful absence washes around our lives. Darkness can creep through the cordon of coping, of theories, of creeds, of optimism that I lay around myself with the pretence of busy-ness and preoccupation. The fear of silence is that it might reveal an awful desolation. 'Save me, God, for the water has risen to my neck. I sink in muddy depths where there is no foothold' (Psalm 69:1–2). Suppose that the lifetime struggle to find my voice is drowned out by silence? What if there is nothing and I am nobody? Could I be swamped by my own loneliness? What if the flood waters engulf me or the depths swallow me up or the pit closes its mouth over me?

My bowl of dough goes into the proving oven. I have pummelled hard as I have let the anxiety of the week be pushed into it. Company arrives. People have started to shed coats, swish their umbrellas like huge waterlogged bats. They greet each other. The kettle is on to make a good dark brew of coffee. There is a surface babble of news. After a while we move to the quiet room and share a poem and a gospel reading. We light a candle to signify that we are free to move into our own space. Some return to the bread table and their conversation, others dive for the newspapers or open books they have brought with them. I decide to stay in the quiet. I am aware that today I feel resentful of noise.

Holiness is often portrayed as a journey. We are on a path, a quest, a trek, climbing a mountain, searching for the Promised Land. We are pilgrims, sojourners, fellow-travellers, marching as to war, we will 'find no rest until we find our rest in Thee'. Yes, but, if I am to 'experience my experience' I cannot always be on the move. I need to stop, take time to process my own thoughts, to search for meaning in the depths of myself. I must rest, let the things that keep me alive start to bubble, to ease myself back into my own shape. I prop myself up with a large cushion on the floor. I am aware that a couple of other people have also stayed in this room. I endeavour to be mindful of them without letting that knowledge make me self-conscious. I struggle to let go of being responsible but it is difficult. I can hear people talking in the other room. I want them to be silent too, to give their tongues a rest for a bit. I try harder not to let my thoughts be intrusive. I know that some of my irritation is not external but comes from inside myself. My head is full of voices too.

I seem to live with so many contradictions these days. With

the desire to develop an inclusive community where all are welcome while also wanting to provide a safe space where people can feel free to expand into their own potential. These two desires are not always compatible. They lead to tensions, sometimes to arguments. I want this city to grow in faith and integrity but there are so many economic and political factors that it seems I will never understand and, if I could, I doubt that anyone would listen to what I had to say anyway. I want this community to be released to find its own voice and to flourish ,yet I still honour and want to remain connected to the tradition which has nurtured me and has ordained me for this role and is so often resistant to change. In church life and in my personal life I seem to live between the twin fears of being abandoned and being overwhelmed. It is a bit like being in the middle of the parted waters of the Red Sea, wondering whether to hang around and be overshadowed by the majesty and grandeur of God or to run for my life. This is a hard place and it needs space for the conversation between the visionary longings of my soul and the physical limitations of my tired feet. If I am going to go in search of a God, who I believe will meet me at the end of my journey, I also need to sit down with him now. To find him keeping night watch on the bridge between something and nothing, between life and oblivion, between destruction and hope, between yesterday and this afternoon. In the beginning God spoke from the boundary between absence and presence, between chaos and form, between isolation and clamour, and the word became flesh and decided to keep us company.

Is holiness about holding onto these contradictions? Paradoxically, learning to abide in God's love is a struggle. For our progress-ridden, outcome-motivated lifestyles the simple act of 'being present' to our lives and to those around us can de-rail our personal ambitions in a spectacular way. The things most likely to throw us off our guard are our encounters with other people. I want to enter into the presence of God but the city and the people in the next room distract me. I have to wait, to hold on, to give it time. I need to smooth the edges of my own irritation with the realisation that I have also been viewed with tolerance and gentleness. Holiness is not a 'desired faith outcome', something that I can achieve if I concentrate hard enough – it is a gentle gift to those who hold and are held. It seems to be about learning to abide in God's love – not in glorious isolation but in the company of others. I sense that holiness is not a state of being but a way of being, a verb rather than a noun. 'I am the way' is both an eternal and an existential statement. I am the way you can live. I am the way to life. I am the way in which you will find yourself. I am the way of becoming something different. I am the transforming way, the gentle way, the attentive way. This is the way, look, see, trust and be upheld, this way is both for you and beyond you. This is the way that it is with God. The Word became flesh and made his home among us ... full of grace and truth.

This is too deep for words, yet we often let the presence or absence of words consume us. It seems we are intent to use words at all costs. Nearly 12 per cent of the population cannot read or write – children under five, those with learning difficulties, the very old, those with poor eyesight and people for whom English is not their native tongue. Yet when people appear at the door of the traditional church the first thing we do is give them a book. When we assume that words are our most natural form of communication, we immediately exclude all those who struggle to hear or write, the deaf, dyslexic, anyone who cannot hold a pen or express their thoughts in abstract concepts.

Words have power and my words can silence other people. From bitter experience, many have knowledge of being silenced. People are silenced in many ways. The abused may be sworn to secrecy. The insecure may not be able to get a word in edgeways. People with little self-confidence may assume they have nothing worth saying. Sometimes society is constructed in such a way that only the powerful will find a voice. In politics, in social reform, in law there are structures that collude with silencing people. This is often manifested in jargon that is wielded as a tool of exclusion by those on the 'inside'. The church is no stranger to this. Laden with jargon and still saturated with a patriarchal frame of reference it has bestowed words on the articulate and theologically educated. As a result worship has often become a spectator sport for the churchgoer or an impenetrable mass of incomprehensible ritual for the uninitiated. Sometimes by choice and sometimes through external pressures the church has pronounced on matters of morality, ethics and justice as if it can speak to every need. It has tended to look for answers rather than give people the tools to live with their contradictions.

I sense that the tools we need are not sledgehammers but hearing aids and spectacles. Tools that help us give attention to our way of interacting, that help us to be with each other in different ways, to see each other with fresh eyes. It is within this dynamic of silence, listening, waiting that it is possible to give voice to our aspirations and struggles. In this way we are released to creative possibilities for mutuality and growth. This is not something that comes easily. It is an intentional process. Someone said to me once, 'If you don't know what an extrovert is thinking you haven't listened; if you don't know what an introvert is thinking you haven't asked.' It is true that some people need to say things to know what it is they are thinking, others need to think things to know what it is they want to say. If we are to live in a creative community we need to be able to find a space for both these requirements without burdening the extroverts with silence or consigning the introverts to endless listening. We are called to discover the dynamic between claiming our own space and listening to others, the ability to negotiate our boundaries, be real about our tolerance levels while continuing to hold the under-confident and shy. Developing a way of being with each other that gives some elasticity to our conversation, engagement and withdrawal, lightness and deepness is a big challenge. I am coming to see that silence is not only about holding the absence of things, but also knowing that it is still possible to speak in the presence of things. It is in the contrast between silence and speech that we find the shadows and sparkle of our lives.

After a while I wander back into the kitchen. Around the table there is a busy chatter. There is Col with a large supply of felt-tip pens drawing a picture of a kite. Carole is making a get well card for someone. David is chuckling over a poem he is writing, Simon is making something out of clay. In the confluence of word and silence comes an outpouring of creativity. There is a lively conversation going on. Mysteriously the desire to make something emerges from our inner conversations and begins to pour out onto blank bits of paper and into friendships; the invisible is becoming visible. My bread has risen spectacularly close to the top of the bowl. It makes us laugh. It needs to be knocked back and shaped into loaves. Together we make a plait of dough and sprinkle it with sunflower seeds. It lies on a large flat baking sheet. The twists expand into each other as the yeast brings texture to the design. It always amazes me how bread knows it is going to be bread. It strikes me that we do not really make bread at all, we simply wait for the ingredients to become the bread that, with time, they come to understand they are intended to be.

Returning to the quiet, I feel easier in myself. I have relaxed into being here. I am no longer trying to make myself be something in the silence. I am learning the intention of silence, to let the silence be silence. Allowing the silence to shape me and letting the inner struggles which form me flow into it helps me to become less irritated and distracted. I realise that irritations and distractions are an integral part of me. I cannot aspire to holiness through denying who I am. I am an embodied human being. I get angry, frustrated, despairing. I have a tendency to get the giggles. I get tired and confused. Sometimes I feel responsible without need. At the moment I am particularly aware of my soggy socks. All of these things are part of who I am. Silence re-creates me when I begin to integrate the whole of this. There is an upholding within the silence in which I am released from doing the holding and become aware that I am being held. Silence understands silence. This is the place where the holding God can inspire us with creative impulses. In which we are being given attention by a larger reality than our small minds can name. Now we may eavesdrop on God's word as it drops like a pebble into a well of eternity. I begin to imagine God's desire for my company. I begin to believe that God waits to pray in me.

Worship begins to take on a different shape. (I note the irony of a Methodist being released from a traditional style of service jokingly referred to as a 'hymn sandwich' and working with the image of a whole loaf!) Maybe for too long, maybe subconsciously, we have imagined a caricature God watching us from on high as a distant presence that needed to be pacified by our subservience and obedience. A God who took note of what we did, not so much to take delight in us but to keep account in some ultimate eternal ledger. We have imagined God needing our worship as if his existence depended upon it and because, by definition, that worship could never be sufficient, we have always been trying to run to catch up. God must somehow be pacified and we have either ended up with a perpetual struggle to be good enough or just opted out. We have often colluded with this myth without realising it. We have said that we believe in a God of justice, mercy and love yet have wanted to draw a line in the sand beyond which we could not pass. Abiding in God's love is a more intimate reality in which we are unable to keep a distance. We have preferred to live with the fear of God abandoning us than with the fear of God overwhelming us. Yes, but a God of love will do neither. Trust in the commitment of a loving God to the relationship with all creation moves forward in a dynamic where we are held but not disempowered.

The holy God is one in which there is an inner relationship of mutuality and difference. The Father neither abandons nor overwhelms the Son, the Spirit lives freely within the dynamic, one with the Father yet blowing all over the place. 'Abiding in God's love' is about trusting this interaction in which we are seen and known and yet free to live and move and have our being. Silence comes in the face of these contradictions. It gives us the space. We can hear the hint of God's desire to relate to all creation. This relationship is not simply about me and my stuff but about the whole world of which I am an important though tiny particle. In this relationship I am both everything and nothing and from out of this contradiction emerges the energy to live. Letting the silence dwell around me allows for some elasticity in my life. I no longer need to live in absolutes but within a creative dynamic that allows me to stretch my imagination to a God of infinite possibilities. Silence holds us in this possibility.

Experiencing the deep, struggling, intensity of silence brings me to another image. One in which I am held in the Creator's imagination, in the mind's eye. The mystery that brings me to worship is that God is mindful of me, that I am re-membered. That the millions of hairs on my head are counted, that I was knit together in my mother's womb, that there has been a desire to love me into life. That the potential of me is seen and the struggles as yet unresolved are held. Holiness is not so much about wholeness, becoming complete or perfect, but about engaging with the whole of who I am, bringing to light the contradictions at the centre of myself. Such an experience comes about not through speech or through lack of it, or indeed by any effort on my part except being prepared to be immersed in God's attentiveness. Through God all things were made, and continue to be made: the poems, the drawings, the conversations, the friendships, the bread, and me. The re-creating of it all happens by waiting in such divine attentiveness.

This, of course, is not a secret. Artists know how to draw on these deep wells, and poets and designers, as does anyone who sings or dances or plays in an orchestra. So too children who blow bubbles, anyone who flies a kite or stares at a baby fresh-born, or looks deeply into a waterfall or climbs a mountain or resolves a difficult equation or looks down a microscope at pollen. All of us have experiences that are beyond words. We may not name the experiences with the name of God but we can perceive them. I assume it does not matter to God to be named or not named. If our creator abides with us then glints and glimmers of creation, touches of delight will continue to crack open the world. Moments of surprise, amazement, exquisite taste and smell, shining things will hint at a giver who hangs around with us, in whose imagination we continue to be made.

If holiness is a reflection of the nature of God, then there is something holy that permeates the whole of creation including ourselves. Holiness is about us being in God as God is in God. If we abide in this reality, then we are held in the palm of God's hand, we are the apple of God's eye, we were loved before we were conceived and nothing can sever us from that love. It is our essence and the means of transfiguration. 'As the Father has loved me, so I love you, remain in my love.' This is an awe-inspiring thought. It can bring us to a place beyond words, a sense of worship. Worship is not something we do but a way of being. It is not a requirement of us or an obligation, it is about perceiving things with fresh eyes, an inspiration to see the familiar faces of our companions in the light of God's involvement with all of us. When all around us is transfigured and transformed by the realisation that God is present in all things, that whatever happens to us we remain in God's love, even in silence, then we are worshipping

For what reason are we to remain in God's love? So that we will have joy, that God and Michael and Col and all the other people who struggle in each other's company will have the potential to make each other joyful. In the kitchen the bread has emerged from the oven, hot and malt. It steams the warm promise of a good lunch. It will be better still spread thickly with jam which will drip off each hunk in a sweet buttery juice. As we return to the quiet room to share what we have made during the morning we are full of anticipation for the feast ahead.

In that anticipation of joy, as we realise that we are held in God's attentiveness, we are reminded of our own inattention to what is going on around us. Did anyone remember to take Michael a cup of coffee? While we have prepared a feast for ourselves we have not been particularly mindful of people, even on our own doorstep, who have no prospect of lunch. We have forgotten that for us fresh bread is an indulgence but for many it is a necessity. We have privatised holiness as a processed Western commodity – we have not remembered that we eat at the expense of others. The remembering can bring us to another sort of silence – a silence of regret or contrition, a silence of being stuck, not knowing how we can make a difference, a silence of helplessness in the face of suffering, a silence that seethes with anger. As we return to the quiet room to share what has come to us during the course of the morning, as we light candles and say our prayers, we bring this to mind. Silence is the place we connect with our own judgement, where we stand without deflection in the light of God's intention for love. Silence leaves us in an exposed place without the defence of words. Sometimes all we can do is remain in the silence.

Standing in silence is both our judgement and our impetus for change. We can know that all is not yet lost, that we can begin to work towards transformation in ourselves and in our city. We can re-embark on the process of behaving with others as we have experienced God holding us in his attention. We can begin by listening. If I think about the people in my life whom I consider to have been holy – most of whom would be amazed at that label being applied to them – I call to mind people who have given me their full attention, as if I was the only person who was important to them at that particular moment. They have shown an interest in me, in what matters to me and how that is influencing my life. They have talked to me about books and insights, shared the flow of a conversation, wanted the best for me, understood something of my struggle without offering a neat set of solutions. They have dwelt with me in the open-endedness of things, have been in solidarity when times have been hard, when relationships have been under strain, when I have not known what to do for the best. They have reflected for me something of God's way with us. They have had committed intentions for justice and truth, they have trusted that goodness can prevail, despite all the things that conspire to bring destruction, they have believed in the possibility for life. They have given me and others the space to find the shape of our own lives. They have challenged those things that have been less than they should be, they have remained silent and hung on in there when we have been confused or bereft of words. They have gone on believing, they have not given up.

So silence calls us back into an assembly of our own contradictions. To keep holding on to each other, remembering each other by name. We return to the struggle of making our relationships more creative. To go on tackling issues. Curiously it is not answers that do this but rather the call back to living out of our own questions, to living out of the dynamic between purpose and senselessness, revelation and confusion. Between the polarities of silence and speech, of darkness and light, of peace and angst, there is generated a potential difference. It is out of a mindfulness of difference that energy is released for change.

My loaf is rather a strange shape, it has twisted and is definitely fatter one end than the other. It sits in a pool of sunflower seeds, it smells wonderful. We take the prayer candles with us from the quiet room and place them in the centre of the big table. Eating is part of worship! Bread, cheese, fruit are on the table. Michael has been persuaded to come upstairs and is already on his second bowl of soup. A conversation begins to unfurl. The police have arrested a number of *Big Issue* vendors in the week for dealing stuff. John had been face down on the floor of the office with his hands handcuffed when last seen. Michael has been struggling to sell the magazine all week because the story has been in the press and the City Council have put up posters about 'not giving money to beggars'. This is a tough issue. Some of us are tired of being harassed for money in the streets, assuming that what is given will just feed a drugs habit. Others want to err on the side of generosity – why should we judge what people need? Some of us feel sorry for the homeless guys, others are irritated. Some think that we compound the problem by being kind, others look for professional agencies as the answer. Michael tells us about how unsafe the hostel feels and how he prefers to sleep outside where he can be free from the threat of fights in a confined space. He does acknowledge that he is often kicked if he stays in a doorway. Some of us are aware that in half an hour we will catch a train back to the suburbs and leave Michael where he is. We are all living out of our own contradictions and that will change us in any number of different ways. We who abide in God's love have to sense that this holding love makes us feel both safe and unsafe. If Michael is held by the same God as we are, then there are implications that will challenge all of us. It would actually be easier to be a valiant pilgrim striding off in search of the Holy Grail than being earthed and present. We face huge challenges because we all live in the purview of the same God. These tensions come out of the silence, and it is the silence that has given them room to grow.

I am aware that today has been full of creative encounter but we have not come up with any shortcuts to answers. We have simply found our way deeper into dilemmas and living this process is hard work. We can only do our best to change the dynamics of the world, shift the balance a bit, keep working within the questions we are given. Yes, but while this is our calling as individuals it is not something to be done alone. Sheep will die if they are kept in isolation, so too the solitary believer. Living out of our experience draws us into questions of belonging and homecoming.

Waiting

We break the bread. It is nearly time to go. There is an easy laughter around the table. Michael has fallen asleep. I have decided to invest in some new shoes. 'Sunday trading?' someone challenges roguishly. I shrug. That is an issue for another day. As I go out of the door I am quickly swept into a crowd going down the hill, seduced by the prospect of the sales. In the shoe shop the sullen weekend assistant reluctantly brings out one pair at a time. There is another sort of silence that refuses to connect with need. My feet are discovered to be of different sizes. Laughter and silence form a centre of finding a new way of relating. Now I put them to the ultimate retail challenge in a shoe shop.

5
Baking

Hanging above Wood Street there is a bomb. It is swaying on a
rope between our building and the Arts Cinema, it is pointing
downwards. We all stand on a chair to look at it. It is swinging
around in the night air and is patchily illuminated by the neon
sign advertising the screening of *Lost in Translation*.
Underneath the bomb three thousand students are on a pub
crawl. It is freshers' week at the university. The students are
shouting and singing. The police horse watches unperturbed,
shifting its weight from one hoof to another. The bomb creaks
backwards and forwards. We are not afraid of the bomb.
Heather tells us that it is part of the Liverpool biennial art
exhibition. The bomb becomes a talking point.

The bombs that fell on Wood Street sixty years ago flattened
it. They flattened Bold Street too, and Church Street and all the
way down to the docks. They flattened the parish church and
the length of Scotland Road. Over seven consecutive nights in
May 1941, 870 tonnes of high explosive and 112,000 fire bombs
were dropped on Liverpool. People were frightened then. Tom
has come to join the bakers today. He is in his seventies, a
widower, white-haired and lonely. He comes every week to
make bread for company and brings stories. He knows
Liverpool better than any of us. He begins to reminisce about
the war. Tom's wife died two years ago today. 'Two years ago
today I lost my wife,' and then a pause, 'I don't know where I
am without her,' he says. That is why Tom comes to make

bread. For company and for someone to listen to his stories and for some time to feel less lost.

The students flood the city in a huge wave. They talk in Irish, London and Korean accents, they appear confident, they are unaware of the bomb. They belong to one of the city's three universities. At the end of the night, if they can remember where they live, they will go home. After a term they will return to where they came from, to their parents, brothers, sisters, girlfriends, for the vacation. After three years they will have become chemists, teachers, engineers, nurses, they will move on with their new partners. They will have to find a home, set up home, track down a place where they feel at home. Maybe they will discover it. Maybe they will spend a lifetime being lost.

I have been sitting at my desk today trying to fill out my membership returns. How many people belong to this church? Who do I count? Do I include the bakers, the worshippers, the people I talk to as chaplain in the shops, Michael? What does it mean to belong? Do I belong here? I certainly do not feel very at home in church these days. What are the signposts that help us recognise where we belong? Who belongs with us? There are so many questions around belonging, identity and homecoming.

Simon is from the Midlands. He arrived in Liverpool with a friend who stole his rucksack and disappeared. He never intended to stay he just did not have enough money to leave. Andrew has lived in Liverpool all his life but divorce dislocated his family. He had to move out of his home and rented a flat for a while. Heather was living in France before she came to work in Lewis's. Both Col's parents have died and two of her brothers are better forgotten. Penny had to sell her home to pay for her gender-change operation. Her friends and family found that hard to understand. She is not really in contact with them now. Marie came to the university as a student and now works in human resources for a local company. She has just put in an offer on a new flat. There is no earthly reason why this random group of humanity should wash up in the same place. They only came to make bread.

We pour oil into the flour in the shape of our initials. We put our name into our bread. And when the dough goes into the proving oven we again mark the bowl with a shape that we will recognise. When the bread is baked, although each of us uses the same basic recipe, every loaf is different. Someone was really agitated this morning because they lost track of their bowl of bread and someone else had started shaping it into loaves. We had to negotiate a compromise. There is a sense of ownership about the bread we make. It is 'our bread' because we are investing our time and energy into making it. It is not cheap bread, like the loaf you can pick up for next to nothing at the local supermarket. This bread costs us time and effort. This bread is worth something because it involves us. Tom and Heather, Andrew and Simon know this. That is why they are so wrapped up with the bread.

Initially this church was just a group of bread-makers, now it is a place where people come purposefully to say their prayers, share their news and tell their stories. Friendships are forming. Out of these friendships interesting connections occur. Marie and Col meet to plan the faith development group, Andrew found Simon a job, and Penny decorated the bread kitchen. Last year Heather and Andrew got married. This is a place of connection between the things we remember from our own stories, and the story of Jesus. There are strong echoes of the Gospel within the storytelling and remembering. This small group of people are not only writing their third pantomime and meeting in the evening to go out for a drink, they also want to pray more, worship more, study the Bible more. We discover a deep desire to converse about what makes life important for us. It is not that we have joined a church and become friends, it is rather that we became friends and a church has appeared.

I have to admit that I have found the emergence of a church a curious thing. I am not amazed that, in my wandering around the city, I met people who wanted to talk with me – this is Liverpool after all and people are prone to talk. I am not even surprised that the conversation often turned to matters of deep concern – relationships, illness, the bombing of Iraq. What I have found curious has been the movement from that towards a desire to pray and worship and, maybe most amazingly, to requests for rites of passage, weddings, baptisms and even a funeral. We meet in rooms above a bookshop. In our biggest room there are two commercial bread ovens. To get to us you must come up four flights of stairs and when you leave you are straight out onto the pavement of one of Liverpool's busiest shopping streets. It does not strike you as the ideal setting for a marriage service. Yet we have had two weddings and two blessings, as well as baptisms and a memorial service for a family where a woman had died leaving teenage children. One bride arrived wearing what my daughter describes as a 'meringue dress' and squashed herself into our miniscule lift with good-hearted giggles. Four months later, when the brain tumour overtook her, I presided at her funeral in the Anglican cathedral with hundreds of mourners including a number of the cast of *Brookside*. While we sang unaccompanied songs in harmony around her grave, and the men and boys shovelled the soft black earth over the coffin, I wondered what the connection is between faith and belonging. Why search for identity among people who feel so lost?

I sense that one clue to engaging with these questions lies in the ability of bread to help us remember. As the warm, homely smell emerges from the hot ovens so memories of childhood are tapped. I have noticed that almost without exception bread-makers begin to talk about memories. They tell stories of making bread with their granny or running to the corner shop for their mothers. Memory brings stories to mind. Imagination triggers the recollection of deep emotions. When these feelings are rediscovered then we begin to remember the whole of us, the forgotten child that lies deep inside, the bruised teenager, the lover, lost or longed for. We begin to remember who we were and how that has led us to becoming who we are now. The story that the bread encourages is a deep one. It touches areas of ourselves we have not recollected for a long time. Our story is part of the way in which we communicate who we are, but it is often too deep to be articulated. We might be frightened of revisiting those deep places; we may be fearful that no one will listen to us or give our story honour. Whether we are able to voice them or not, memories lead to story. In whatever way these stories are expressed they bring about a conversation either privately within ourselves or outwardly with others. Such a conversation leads to inner and outer connections and connections lead to the discovery of our identity. Our 'story' is the way in which we make connections between ourselves and our experience. Our story tells us who we are.

Jesus saw a man born blind. The un-seeing man was waiting. He was a beggar. Jesus spat in the mud and spread it on his eyes. It was the Sabbath day. The authorities were trying to catch out Jesus. They wanted to trick him into disclosing his identity. Was he saying he was the Son of God? In order to discover this they had to establish whether the man Jesus was supposed to have healed had in fact been blind. To prove the identity of Jesus they had to prove the identity of the beggar. The parents were brought. 'This is indeed our son and indeed he was born blind,' they said. Implicit in this gospel story is the story of a family struggling with their blind son. They are wrestling with the implication that somehow they were responsible for this. They articulate their own anxiety – whose sin has caused this to happen? In their desire to make sense of their own life story the blind man's family are confronted not only by their own self doubt but also by a theology of authority and blame. The experience of their son's blindness has led them into a multitude of questions about themselves and their relationship with God. Confronted by religious purists trying to prove a point all they can do is return to their own experience. 'He is our son, he was born blind, his eyes have been opened; we don't know how.' When the theology does not fit the experience there are only two options, deny the experience or change the theology.

The man was brought back. The religious authorities were desperate to prove that Jesus was an impostor. The man replied, 'Whether he (Jesus) is a sinner or not I do not know. What I do know is that I was blind and now I see.' The man is challenging the authorities by claiming the authenticity of his own experience, 'I was blind, now I see.' The traditional story of salvation is not fitting the facts. There is a collision between Scripture and experience. The story crashes into the present tense. Now we see the theology shifting. If the experience of blindness to sight is irrefutable then there are implications for the identity of Jesus. There has been a transition, a transformation that is the pivot of the story. It turns things around so that we have to look at them from a different direction. We can no longer refer to a 'blind man' but to a 'seeing man'. When the seeing man recognises that he belongs within his own story it dawns on him that he now also belongs within the story of Jesus. In order to make sense of what has happened to him he must also recognise who it is that he has encountered. The encounter is not only transforming the physical reality of his life, it is also transforming his frame of reference. He is moved into asking different questions. He is also challenging the people around him into asking different questions. Instead of asking, 'Does your experience belong within this tradition?' they are being moved to ask, 'How does this experience change our tradition?' When they begin asking a different question, when the perceived cause of the man's blindness is transferred from being his own or his parent's fault to being wrapped up in the identity of Jesus, then there is trouble. The story of Jesus is involved with the story of the seeing man in a way that is about to change a whole way of looking at the world. When that reality breaks in we all begin to see each other for the first time. Connection leads to identity and identity leads to a new way of seeing.

As we watch the bread through the glass doors of the oven

we see a change. The white, unstable lumps of risen dough are placed in their tins and slotted onto the shelves. We place them gently in the centre of the oven. If they bump into the ledges above them or to the side they will soon collapse. They rise fractionally more but the fierce heat soon stops the yeast and the loaves take on a firmer shape. The crust begins to brown, the steam is driven out. The bubbles are caught within the texture and the dough is transformed into bread. We leave the loaves in the oven and go through to the quiet room to say our prayers. From the windows in the quiet room we look down on the roofs of Bold Street. At the top of our street is the shell of St Luke's. During the Second World War the guts of this church were taken out by a bomb. Only the walls remain. This skeleton of a building holds the empty memory of war. It provides a damaged sanctuary for rough sleepers. Our story, the city's story, the gospel story are held side by side in the view from our window. The connection between them makes a conversation. Tom says he remembers the night that St Luke's was bombed. He remembers the man opposite who refused to go down into the shelter but stood in his doorway to watch the incendiaries land along the dock road and onto the roofs of the neighbouring buildings. Tom remembers how it felt to be there then. He is still trying to make sense of all the things he has lost. The stories he tells are the threads of memory that connect him to his past and help him claim who he is now. Yes, but despite all that he has lost he is still Tom.

Stories connect us through time and they also connect us with each other. We begin to identify ourselves in the company of other people. 'No branch can bear fruit by itself, it must remain in the vine. Neither can you bear fruit unless you remain in me.' Not every group of friends makes a church. Sometimes they make a golf club or a school reunion. So why is it that a church is emerging from the bread-making friendships and what are the hallmarks by which we recognise it is a church? Conversation is a two-way thing. It unfurls when people meet within the to and fro of storytelling. It comes from the empathy between speaker and listener. It is a gift. Yet it is a gift that we are inclined to take lightly because it is also a risk. We may tend to allow conversation to skim the surface rather than engage with the deep resonances of our souls. Often we dare not risk the vulnerability of such exposure. Authentic conversation requires unconditional regard for the life of another person, openness, a willingness to meet simply within our humanity.

Connection leads to change, to transfiguration. The bread conversation is different from the conversation in the school reunion or the golf club because it has an intention. Not only does it have the intention of a non-judgemental encounter between equal human beings but we also intend to have a conversation with the gospel story. This is not the hard sell of power-based mission. There is no hidden agenda here – we will not be nice to people in order to enter into some way to convert them. Heaven forbid. We simply intend to let the Gospel rest with us. It does not look like much. It looks like a group of people making bread, engaged on a task, taking some time for quiet and then eating a simple lunch. But this intentional conversation brings a sense of belonging, a connection and out of that comes a transfiguration of the ordinary. Suddenly we begin to see things with fresh eyes.

This is a deceptively simple process. It takes some holding. A Christian conversation requires non-manipulative facilitation. There need to be some rules of engagement – confrontational questions, personal remarks, intrusive curiosity, however well meaning, need to be redirected. There have to be clear signals. People need to perceive that it is permitted to engage or disengage according to personal choice. Everyone should have the attention they desire without diminishing the attention given to others. It needs empathetic, wise facilitation. And we often get it quite wrong. In a room of needy people it is easy to allow the most articulate or demanding to dominate. We can tend to think that people with visible needs are those with most needs. We can make assumptions that put people on the spot. We have had to learn to apologise. It is very demanding. We not only need eyes in the backs of our heads but also the intuition and insight to hold people in true regard. As we come to see people with all their complexity and wonder then we are all changed. Transfiguration leads to transformation. It requires a profound trust in the process. Despite all this apparent lack of evangelical drive we are all transformed here.

It is hard to describe it but we can see it with our own eyes. Simon has just completed his first week of work. He is pleased and tired. It has been hard for him. A few months ago he was leading the chaotic existence of a *Big Issue* vendor. He is still fragile, vulnerable, prone to being knocked back. But he is changing. He is being changed, not by us, but in our company. He is beginning to live his own story. His company is changing us too. Transformation comes through recognition. It is not only that the blind man has been given his sight, he has also become somebody. He has been seen. The authorities suddenly needed to know who he was. As a blind man he was nothing, no one even knew his name, but as someone recognised by Jesus he became part of a bigger picture. When he is noticed, the blind man becomes confident, he stands up. He faces up to the authorities and challenges them, 'Now that is remarkable, you don't know where he (Jesus) comes from yet he opened my eyes.' Not only does the seeing man start to recognise the importance of his own story in the light of God's story, he also starts to change the bigger story. Like the seeing man, Simon is beginning to perceive his own significance. He is beginning tentatively to stand on his own two feet. He tells us about his first week at work. We recognise some of the importance of the story we are hearing. We appreciate some of the struggles that Simon has had in facing his new job. We know that it might not work out for him. We come to understand that this struggle will make a difference to all of us. We begin to see how Simon and the bakers together are involved in God's story. Transformation is not necessarily about making changes but about seeing ourselves and others in a different way. Really seeing and loving the essence of what makes someone who they are, loving the essence of ourselves as individuals and as a community.

The conversations around the bread table also lead to conversations with traditions, with assumptions, with political or religious dogma. How does the experience challenge these? If you are a gay man and a Muslim it is hard to find a place to be yourself. If you are also an asylum-seeker and your brother is dying from AIDS where would you go to say your prayers? Where could you find a place to be yourself for a while? A place where you could be both known and yet anonymous, a place of acceptance rather than interrogation? When looked at from the context of a strict Islamic regime the UK might give the impression of being tolerant towards a variety of sexual orientations, but the combination of language difficulties, asylum legislation and entrenched faith perspectives can make hospitality a scarce commodity. It is often easier for asylum-seekers to remain invisible than to risk being discovered. As I write I am aware that I have someone in mind that I cannot name. Someone who cannot live his own name. Someone who cannot earn money or register with a doctor or settle into any employment although he works hard and wants to do so legally. Someone who wants to pray in the light of day and be himself before God. Someone who lives in the half-light of society. Someone who deserves to be seen. Someone whose experience challenges every aspect of what we might consider to be traditional theology. Someone who will be executed if he goes home. Someone who has already been in fear of his life in this city. For the purposes of this story we will call him 'Ahmed'. We are challenged to work with our assumptions in every aspect of this encounter. It seems to me that the only way into understanding is to converse. In this conversation we must all risk losing our settled certainties and set out from home. As we listen to our own fears we are enabled to perceive the person within the issue. Jesus says to the seeing man, 'For judgement I have come into the world so that the blind will see and those who see will become blind.' These are harsh words directed at those who profess religious certainties and cannot spot the work of God in front of their own eyes. When we converse we open up the whole of ourselves to being transformed. In this exchange, as we recognise the Divine image in each other, we may find the way to let our traditions live.

The way is not a blind fumbling with pluralism, postmodernism and endless possibilities. Its hallmark is the intention to see one another and to love one another. The intention is not to transform people – bring about conversion under our own steam with some pretence of friendliness. The intention is to engage genuinely with ourselves while honouring the difference of our neighbour. It is this open-eyed engagement that makes the difference. True conversation is not so much about agreeing or about having all the answers but about seeing each other differently. It is about hearing each other's questions and noticing when experience and tradition rub up against each other. The hermeneutical conversation between Scripture, reason, tradition and experience is an organic, living, transforming process.

We stand at the window of the oven and watch the bread. It is always wonderful. Even five years on from the start of this project I am still capable of being amazed by the bread. Sometimes we have groups of people here who mix the ingredients in the wrong order, are in too much of a rush to wait for the dough to rise properly; on warm days the yeast can get overactive, on cold days we work with unyielding lumps of mixture. Sometimes we fear the outcome of a frantic morning's work yet the bread becomes bread. We are learning to trust in a process that we do not control. When you stand and watch the bread cooking you can recognise that this trusting of process itself brings transformation. Not only does transformation come through recognition but recognition comes through transformation. Living the process is what makes the difference.

For years Penny was a car mechanic. She was born with a man's body but a woman's identity. During the first half of her life she thought God had played a cruel trick. Now she has found her home within a woman's body. She is employed helping people like her, who are considered different, find their way into employment. She also advises the police with their anti-discrimination practice. She is the church property steward. One year after Penny was born as a woman she was baptised at the bread church. What light does this shed on the words of Jesus, 'unless a man be born again ...'? She has re-found faith in God as she has found faith in herself. When Penny was baptised we made a well. It was actually a large basin of water cleverly disguised as a well. Beside the well there was a deep blue cloth and a pile of pebbles. We started the service here. Penny told us some of her story. Penny's story is amazing, difficult, painful. There are moments when it looked as if she would not survive. After we had heard Penny's testimony we read the account in chapter four of St John's gospel where Jesus asks the woman at the well for water. 'Who's asking?' she wants to know. Jesus does not reply directly but as he offers her living water he tells her all kinds of secret things about herself and her relationships. He recognises her. He hears the woman's longings to meet the Messiah. Then she recognises him. We hear that many Samaritans from that city believed in him because of the woman's testimony: 'He told me all that I ever did.' Being seen, recognised, known to be present in our own story, seeing that we are present in Jesus' story can bring belief. Jesus offers the woman living water before she believes. The transformation is in the conversation. Identity, faith, recognition, transformation – there is a mysterious connection. Once I was not seen and then I was seen. Once I could not see and now I see.

Recognition and transformation are so deeply linked. When we are seen as ourselves, then we are free to be ourselves and we are freed to make choices about our lives. When we make choices about our lives we can become ourselves and we are able to recognise the wonder of other people. Belief in ourselves and belief in God are wrapped up together. We understand that God believes in us when we experience other people believing in us. Jesus heard that they had thrown out the seeing man and he went in search of him. When Jesus found him he said, 'Do you believe in the Son of Man?' 'Who is he, sir?' the man asked. 'Tell me so that I may believe in him.' The seeing man begins to ask living questions. He wants to hear how he fits into the story. Jesus said, 'You have now seen him; in fact, he is the one speaking with you.' Then the man said, 'Lord, I believe!' That is the remarkable thing about Jesus: he sought the man even after he had been thrown out. Jesus was not content that the blind man should be able to see, he desired for the seeing man to be able to understand. Jesus met the man who could now see and in the seeing was the believing.

So, do belief and belonging go together? The church has assumed that they do. At the Methodist baptism and confirmation service when people declare their belief in God as Father and Jesus Christ as Lord then they are 'received into membership'. When we believe in Christ we say that we belong to Christ. And when we belong to Christ then we belong to the church. We try to learn more about God and the church and the ethics that inform our choices. That is important, but do we also try to learn more about ourselves? How does faith help us to discover the essence of ourselves? As Penny has shown the bread-makers, the discovery of our own story is an essential part of discovering ourselves to be part of God's story. We may have traditionally thought of faith as the precursor to belonging but the bread-makers are discovering that a sense of belonging may just as readily lead to belief. The blind man is seen, he is addressed, he is given sight, his identity is established, he believes, he sees. You have been seen, you have been addressed, you have been known, your identity unfolds, you believe, you see. That is the process.

Process is about transition. It becomes clearer now why the

key points of connection between belonging and believing are rites of passage. As we engage with the human experience of transition – between jobs, homes, identities, relationships – so there is a human need to mark this transition with an event. In the same way as the branches of a vine are grafted onto a root, so people flourish as they reconnect with the life-giving sap of their story and the story of faith. Finding ourselves is not simply a solitary journey towards self-fulfilment: it is our movement towards a homecoming to the source of all life. We may not yet have found our final destination but we need to honour the movement towards a connection with the essence of ourselves, the essence of all that we can become in the company of others, of all that we are intended to be. Rites of passage are signposts to that connection. They are way-markers.

As usual, I discover that I am asking the wrong question. It no longer matters how many people say they belong to the church so that I can prove that there is life in a flagging institution. Instead of 'Who belongs to this church?' I need to ask 'To whom does this church belong?' I suppose the answer is that we are working it out. We know that we cannot talk glibly about our faith in a neat set of certainties. Learning to love as Jesus loves takes us to the very limits of our wit and understanding. Many people will live this process without having anything whatsoever to do with a church, traditional or otherwise. Some will try to find a home in church and be excluded. We must learn not to expect everyone of faith to fit into the church's story – it is too confined a space for many people's experiences to be held. Those of us who still hang on in there need to keep letting others' experiences blow the tradition apart. I do not find many guidelines on transgender issues in the gospel of St John. What I do find is a way of encounter in which our stories as individuals and as a community and God's story can interact. I want to own it as a life-giving interaction.

Belonging to the gospel story is not transposing ourselves

into first-century Palestine and believing everything applies to us as it did then. The Gospel of the present tense is a call to find meaning in the story of our lives and in the places where we live. For us bakers it means we have to work at what it means to be people of faith in Liverpool here and now. As our city works on discovering what it might mean to be 'City of Culture' we discover how it is also grappling with its own story. That is why it has slung a bomb above Wood Street. We are aware that this city's story is not just about the Beatles and football and art exhibitions, but also about slavery, war and exploitation. The experience of being in the presence of all this is our challenge to live authentically in the light of the Gospel. The hallmarks of that authenticity are the conversations, connections and transformations that we begin to witness with our own eyes. This discovery will draw us into dialogue with the author, designer, architect and artist, everyone who is telling a story here and now. We are also being called into dialogue with the gospel story. It is a conversation that will engage us in the struggle of living our own questions. It is that interaction that will change us. A vine is a living thing.

Experiencing our experience of belonging, believing, faith and doubt are all linked somehow with our story and the story of the place, but there is more than this. Some days we can see signs of transformation with our own eyes, hear echoes of something else going on, get glimpses and flavours of the Kingdom, but we cannot force the process. We have to learn to wait and wonder as we live out of our own silences and questions. If I am to be real about all this I have to acknowledge my own tolerance levels and frustrations. It is impossible to be limitless in accepting diversity and struggling with questions. If I shelve feelings and emotions they will surely reappear in the morning.

For now the bread is tapped out of its tins onto the cooling racks. As each loaf is turned upside down the steam is released and whooshes upwards towards the ceiling. Tom opens the window. The bomb is wet with rain. Heather is reading the brochure for the art exhibition. 'It says the bomb represents a seed, the potential for regeneration that follows destruction,' she enlightens us. The students are moving on. I hope they remember their way home.

6

Cooling

Coming into the city on MerseyRail with my elder son this morning someone pulled the communications cord. The train juddered to a halt and an announcement was made that we would be delayed. There was a collective groan in the carriage and a general resignation to the ways of lads that mess about on trains. Rob and I exchanged glances. No one thought it was a real emergency – a terrorist attack or a sudden death – they just moaned about 'the youth'. Arriving late I find Michael being antagonised by a passing workman who is telling him to get off his f... backside and get a f... job. Standing beside Michael I tell the workman, who seems at least twice my size, to butt out of it. I brew Michael a cup of tea and we talk for a while. He shrugs his shoulders as if to say, 'That's just how it is.' I climb the stairs and dump my stuff in the meeting room. On the table lies a discarded flyer from the Merseyside Stop the War Coalition that says, 'Troops out now, save Ken Bigley'. Ken Bigley, the kidnapped Liverpool construction worker in Iraq, had his throat cut yesterday. The protest is too late. I put the flyer in the bin.

For all these reasons I start the day feeling angry. I plot to loosen the bolts on the scaffolding where the workman is painting windows, I devise a plan to single-handedly assassinate President Bush, I want to stand with my sons at the station and tell the old bats that not all young people on trains pull communication cords. I sit and seethe with my cup of coffee. When I answer the phone I sound like a doctor's receptionist on flu vaccine day. I am with the Psalmist when he writes, 'Arise, Lord, confront them and bring them down; save me from the wicked; make an end of them with your sword. With your hand, Lord, make an end of them; thrust them out of this world from among the living' (Psalm 17:13–14). As I calm down I become annoyed at my ability to calm down. I am adept at squashing my inner fury; it seems my anger often changes nothing but my mood.

At prayer time we read the passage in St John's gospel (chapter 5) where Jesus heals the lame man at the pool. The story goes that an angel stirs up the water from time to time and the first person to get themselves into it is miraculously healed. Now all the people waiting for the angel are either blind or lame, so it seems to me that this promise of healing is rather a mean trick. If you could see the waters being whisked up you could not reach them, and if you were in position to reach them you could not see when to make a move. Thirty-eight years and no one to help him left the guy in the story understandably exasperated. Yet he continued sitting hopefully by that impossible pool.

Jesus, on the other hand, was not sitting around waiting. He had been so annoyed with the money-changers wheeling and dealing in the Temple that he had thrown their tables over and accused them of being a den of thieves. And when he appears in the story by the pool he is antagonising the authorities by encouraging the healed individual to carry his mat on the Sabbath day. Jesus apparently deliberately goes around provoking these indignant reactions, reactions that could so easily move into retribution and violence. He sees something and in his engagement with it throws the presuppositions of the onlookers into total confusion. Their anger is the reaction to experiences that do not make sense.

If we are to 'experience our experience' then we will experience all kinds of experience. Experience does not get filtered before it impacts on our senses. Some experience brings with it a sense of injustice, discrimination, violence and hatred. In the light of this we should expect to be angry. Anger is not the experience, it is the reaction to an experience. But where does that anger lead us? Often it leads us into violence – either outwardly and physically or inwardly and mentally. Is there any way to break out of these destructive circles of retribution and bloodshed? Should we stand in powerless solidarity with the powerless, or does that simply collude with a victim mentality? How should we challenge the inherent violence in all of us? Much has been written about this in a global sense, in response to September 11th and the continuing facing of violence with violence. This violence may be considered to emanate from desire, covetousness, the invasion of territory. But what does that mean in the light of trying to live in a different way today, here, within this community? Does this small bread-making enterprise have any light to shed on the anger we encounter when global, political or sociological influences impact negatively on the life of our neighbourhood?

The bread is tipped upside down onto wire racks to cool off. It is scorching hot and sounds hollow when tapped. We open the window to let the steamy vapours escape, covering the loaves with crisp white tea towels to prevent dust settling on them. We sit and talk. We remember the Lent workshops a few months ago when we were encouraged to enact the story in Luke's gospel in which Jesus reads from the synagogue scroll about Jubilee. We each took the part of someone in the story. One of us became a prisoner and cowered under a chair, someone else a blind person and walked around knocking into things. Carole and I were the Jewish authorities, not impressed by what was going on. Tony took the part of Jesus. Tony quickly got into role. In his forthright Scottish way he pointed an accusing finger at the prisoner, 'Oi what are you doing under there, stop skulking in prison, get yourself out of here.' And then he turned on the blind man and told him to stop pratting about – 'Open your eyes and get on with your life.' At the end of the morning we were all exhausted. We sat drinking coffee and talking about how the role-play had made us feel. Carole and I not only had trouble with Tony in our role as religious authorities, the real Carole and Barbara were also anxious that he might go back to his *Big Issue* pitch being as assertive as the Jesus in the play. He put his hands on his hips and, looking us straight in the eye, 'My Jesus is not the same as your Jesus' he said with the inflection of extreme irritation.

My childhood taught me that it was naughty to be angry; Tony's taught him it is normal to be angry. He gets put into prison from time to time to cool off after some confrontation in the street; I get myself into an internal knot, bark down the phone and then feel guilty about it. Michael shrugs his shoulders as if he must always be a victim, the workman swears to alleviate the pressure of his own uncertainties and the old ladies on the train scapegoat people they do not understand. Jesus provoked his own violent death, chucked the money-lenders out of the Temple, swiping the table legs from under them. When it comes to anger we are walking contradictions but truth to tell we all get angry in one way or another. We are all capable of producing more heat than light. Anger is an experience we all experience. The dilemma is what are we to do with it?

I have a problem with Jesus being so angry. I have taken a long time to understand that being angry is allowed. At an early age I swallowed the 'no one likes an angry woman' motif. I need to acknowledge the healthiness of anger while not becoming its victim. For me this is a problem that originates in my experience of being a woman in a world where male violence seems so often to overrule. From survivors of abuse on my own doorstep to the plight of Ken Bigley, the power of violence appears to override the path of gentleness. I feel ill equipped to deal with my own anger or anyone else's. Worse still, I want to be a person of faith but religion can be the weapon by which the quiet are silenced, the disempowered are annihilated. I want to believe that peace can prevail but violence appears to be endemic. What is 'the way' that the anger of Jesus tells us about? Is Jesus simply another man asserting his position at the expense of others? How can women and men both claim their anger without entering into the vicious circles of destructive violence or being violated by those who use anger as a means of power? How can I be real about how I feel about Michael and Ken Bigley and the train but express that reality in a different way? How can we find the route by which anger is separated from destruction? We can often feel as paralysed as a person who cannot walk waiting for a person who cannot see to tell them when to move.

Maybe we can turn the tables on our patterns of reacting if we ask what Tony meant when he said, 'My Jesus is not the same as your Jesus' I suspect he was not deliberately making an in-depth theological point, rather referring us to a relationship. He was talking about the relationship he is discovering with God as he sells the *Big Issue* at the end of the street. Tony, Carole and I do not have the same relationship with Jesus because we do not have the same experience. As Tony experiences his own experience so he encounters the God of that experience. I am beginning to see that this is why Jesus was so angry in the Temple. The authorities were denying his experience of God as his Father. When we deny the experience of others as being valid experience then anger erupts. Anger marks the threshold between contradictory experiences, 'My Jesus is not your Jesus.' Are we going to fight about it as if our own experience is the only valid experience or are we going to enter the upside-down world of the Kingdom of God? You can talk all you like over a cup of coffee about being upside down in some detached fashion but that is not the same as dangling from your seat head down on the Blackpool Big One. The upside-down world of which Jesus speaks is that sort of whole-body experience.

Possibly the group of people who provoke me most are other Christians. That is because they threaten me most. All my life I have lived with people telling me why I am not a Christian. Because I am a Methodist, because I am an ordained woman, because I believe that gay people are behaving as naturally within their sexual orientation as straight people, because I do not choose to use the language of being 'born again', because I believe there is truth in Islam, because I am not entirely convinced of the authority of the Pope. I jump up and down in religious indignation. I resort to arguing in the realms of doctrine. I devise secret plans to blow up the Vatican and encourage the Church of England to split over matters of sexuality. I have not yet discovered Tony's honesty in saying, 'My Jesus is not the same as your Jesus.' Anger could be the threshold of saying that, I could be irritated enough to enter a dialogue but I prefer to entrench myself in my own stance. I am reluctant to allow the experience enough space to inform the argument. I would prefer to live by religious certainties – albeit liberal certainties – than by face-to-face encounter. It is easier that way. It is easier for us to say that we cannot enter into troubled water rather than jump in from the edge. It is a tough decision to roll up the bed of our limiting yet familiar circumstances and to walk into a different relationship.

A few weeks ago Peter came to make bread. He was on his mobile phone when he walked through the door and greeted us with the words, 'I don't want to be here, I don't like bread and I don't want to make any.' There was a room full of bakers, Peter and the other vendors were late, we had already sat down for a break and we were pushing ourselves to be welcoming. Peter sat at the table and texted his girlfriend on his phone. No amount of persuasion could encourage him to wash his hands and make bread. Eventually, with exasperation on my part I had one last try. 'Tell you what,' I said, 'if I fill up one of these bread bowls with water and bring it over here with some soap, would you wash your hands then?' To be honest I did not anticipate that he would agree. I was muttering under my breath as I turned towards the sink to fill the bowl. I confess to doing it with bad grace. I was tired, he was idle, I suspected that I was a soft touch. Still chuntering I returned to the table with the bowl and waited for him to wash – his hands were ingrained with the long-term grime of many rough sleepers. He took his time. I waited. Then with what I can only describe as a wicked grin he looked me in the eye and asked, 'Are you going to wash my feet as well?'

I laughed. I laughed at the situation and at myself, at my own presumption of power, my assumption that my Jesus was the only Jesus around. When we encounter each other in this way we can cross a threshold that anger has given to us. We can cross a threshold in different ways, into violence or into a profoundly challenging encounter with another's humanity. There needs to be space to decide how to engage, how to choose the way.

Jesus did something strange after he had cured the lame man. First he disappeared into the crowd, which seems quite reasonable especially in the light of the controversy he had provoked by instructing the man to pick up his bed and carry it on the Sabbath. But after a while he finds the man again and assures him of his own forgiveness. The man then knows Jesus by name and goes back to the authorities and tells them it was in fact Jesus that had cured him. Why does Jesus do that? Why is he not simply content to have melted into the crowd?

There is something about this engagement, dis-engagement and re-engagement that is key to the way that Jesus is relating. He is not avoiding controversy but he is taking time to enter it and to leave it and then return to it. There is a space between the anger and the encounter that strengthens the relationship. The cured man is not simply the subject of the story but is now an active participant in the story. He can enter into the controversy himself. In this new relationship between the walking man and Jesus there is an engagement and a space, contact and reflection, annoyance and walking away. As my anger with Peter was given space on the way to the sink and in my choice to return with the bowl a relationship was formed between us, a relationship that at first Peter comprehended more clearly than me. It was in the space between us, in the difference, in the anger, that the tables got turned. And it was Peter that turned them.

Anger can be the threshold to a new way of relating, but we all need some space to let off steam. When Peter eventually made bread he thumped it so hard that the next day the table legs needed tightening. We learned later that he had been in the *Big Issue* foyer when the police had raided a couple of weeks ago and had spent quite a while flat on the floor. That is not unusual; it is pretty much the story of Peter's life. I realise now the immense step he took when he came to make bread with us. All of us feel threatened in someone else's space. All of us feel defensive when our space is invaded. Anger and defensiveness are not opposites. They are our physical defence against threat. As we wrestle with our physical adrenalin-prompted response there is a re-engagement with our own physicality. We are embodied human beings and our spirituality is not something that floats above our heads in some detached cloud, it is incarnate.

Bread is a good reminder of our embodiment. It has come to represent the basic requirements of nutrition. Whatever disaster befalls us, if we at least have some bread then we can survive. That is why when there is any kind of crisis – even a petrol crisis – people's first reaction is to empty the supermarket shelves of loaves. That is why wars are fought about bread. When you come down to it we are all only one pay packet away from Tony or Michael or Peter or the people of Somalia or Iraq. Our existence is more fragile than we care to admit. Bread symbolises the bottom line. The bread line. Without bread for ourselves or our children we will all fight. At this point we are all equally angry. That is why peace comes about only by the long, slow commitment of aid workers to sharing resources and our long-term commitment to engage with issues of social exclusion by sitting down around the same table sharing the loaves we have made. This is a small, long-term project and always so vulnerable to the side swipe of belligerent certainties. We have to go on believing that this bread belongs to everyone. That it is always possible to be better at sharing it. That at this table the poorest have the place of honour – not because of some magnanimous generosity on the part of the powerful but because that is where the embodied Jesus is most apparent. This is subversive. It turns upside down assumptions of both to politics and economics; this is why Jesus said 'I am the bread'. Bread is a good reminder that God is incarnate.

Tony has been making the soup today. He does become quite territorial of his pan of soup. He has had a group of people chopping potatoes and carrots, someone has been sent to the vegetable market for a turnip and some leeks. Several pints of stock and some onions and lentils have also been lobbed into the huge saucepan. I am allowed to stir it but even that is supervised quite closely. The mixture gets thicker and thicker and half has to be decanted into another pan and water added to each. Some joke is cracked about feeding the five thousand. Tony glares at them and continues undaunted. At lunchtime we sit together around our huge table to eat. Soup and bread are taken down to Michael on the doorstep. Tony is congratulated on his recipe and encouraged to let someone else have a turn at soup-making next time. We eat together because we are tired and need to replenish our energy levels. We are running out of steam. All of us need this lunch. We lift our spoons to begin when one of the *Big Issue* vendors who is visiting us objects, 'I thought this was supposed to be a church,' he says. Inside myself I am thinking 'Now what?' but I ask, 'Yes, is there something you want to say?' To my surprise he puts his hands together and begins to say grace. He says thank you for the food and then leads us in a 'Hail Mary' (Methodists struggling at this point!) and an 'Our Father'. Carole and I exchange glances across the table. We know that we have just witnessed the breaking in of something important, we could call it 'the Kingdom'.

Cooling

There is not much time to reflect on this because as we sit and talk there are two people around the table really winding each other up. We are aware that there is quite likely to be a flaring of tempers at some point. We sit strategically between the parties concerned ready to field any comments aimed to irritate. Not everyone can read the social cues that indicate it is time to back off. Sometimes it needs a third party to intervene. Sitting in the middle of things, holding the space between people, is tough. It requires a certain amount of ruthless honesty and the ability to know when to laugh. Sometimes we get it right and sometimes we just make things worse. I have on occasion stood physically between two people that nearly came to blows. I am small enough and command enough respect within the community to get away with such a manoeuvre but there is an art in knowing when to do that and when to call the police. Putting your body in the same place as the anger is not recommended for enhancing life survival rate. Jesus did it and they crucified him.

I am not greatly attracted to martyrdom although I do not rule out the fact that there are some causes for which it is worth dying. I am more attracted to the concept that there are some causes for which it is worth living (even if you die in the process). One of these is a commitment to what the politicians call social inclusion and what the theologians call grace. The grace we say before meals is not so much the hasty chant of some mantra that precedes a good tuck in, rather it is an act of remembering that we are fed by the grace of God – what we Methodists affirm as prevenient grace, that is, a belief in the knowable, unconditional love of God for everybody. That is a grace that, seeing all people as worth loving, sees all people as worth feeding. Grace that goes ahead of us, that is to be discovered rather than earned. We have not deserved it any more than we have earned this meal. It is an act of generosity and as such is to be both enjoyed and shared. This shifts the power in the concept of social inclusion from the powerful giving access to the disempowered to the belief that we are all included through the equality of God's love. We are invited to sit down together at the same table by the same host.

Saying grace before we eat means we have to pause. Carole and I are given a moment to realise the significance of what is going on. When Jesus is involved with the crowd that has gathered to stone a woman 'caught in adultery' he deliberately does not catch anybody's eye but he does cause a pause in the proceedings by writing in the sand. There in the moment before the lobbing of the first brick there is a moment to allow anger to be deflected. This does not necessarily mean that the anger will not turn to violence, it is just that the way of gentleness is given space to have a chance. So, Jesus takes his time. He stands in the middle of the protagonists. He challenges the crowd, 'Let the one who is without sin throw the first stone.' Jesus himself is the only one without sin. He is the only one entitled to throw the stone, everyone else is on the wrong side of the line. Only he can throw it – and he chooses not to. He puts his body at the centre of the controversy. He makes the crowd hold fire and through the encounter her life is returned to her. Without God's grace everyone is the wrong side of the line. Being a woman caught in adultery in the time of Jesus is not far removed from being a gay Muslim asylum-seeker today. The penalty remains the same. The angry mob remains the same. And we are all on the wrong side of the line. Not one of us is in the place to throw the stone. That is why it is so important to locate ourselves in the space between anger and action – to let the choice of the action move from violence to gentleness.

But this is a tough call. As Marie asked in exasperation one day, 'Why is it that the excluded are so difficult to include?' Where we have failed most spectacularly is with some people with mental health issues. We can get so far and then we get stuck. We get stuck when the line between truth and reality becomes indistinct. We have found the demands of bipolar people particularly difficult. We struggle when people become too needy or make false promises to other vulnerable members of the community. We have found that some people with mental health issues have swung between exalting and rubbishing what is going on around them. Sometimes their delusions have brought confusion and guilt to others. We have agonised long and hard as to whether we can be totally inclusive of people whose irrationality has meant that truth becomes too slippery to hold. We have not so much excluded some people with mental health issues as been unable to help them to feel included. That has often left all of us feeling frustrated and angry, particularly with ourselves. Maybe the call to explore the area of spirituality and mental health could open up a different space. So far for us it seems to have been a line we have been unable to cross. If we are to talk about the upside-down nature of the Kingdom being a 'whole body' experience then that presumably has to include the mysteries of the mind – it is just that we have not worked out just how to do it yet. I hope that these people will stay angry with us for long enough to help us not to give up.

How is it possible to find the space in which anger can be expressed? There is so little emotional or physical space to be real about how we feel. Often the result is a bursting out of frustration or, possibly worse, a resignation to being a victim. In our local paper the young people of the area are described as 'youths' and usually in the same breath as 'antisocial behaviour order'. Michael, Peter and Tony know only too well what it is like to be spat on and sworn at. Violence against racial minorities is prevalent, through street crime or blatant discrimination. How can we find space to see each other? Making bread together is such a small thing but for those of us who are involved it does give some time to be ourselves and to see each other, to talk with each other, be angry together, celebrate some of the things that give us pleasure and to find some room to ease our own emotional logjams. We are not always comfortable in each others' company but at least we are working on being together in a different way. As we get to know each other we are learning how to be gentle but it is not at all easy.

We know a lot more about stepping across the threshold of anger into violence than we do about stepping into gentleness. Gentleness sounds a weak word. It may seem to imply submission but on the contrary it is not so much a passive response to anger but an alternative action. It is a dis-arming way of being because it will not meet violence with violence. It is about standing firm, holding fast, defusing the tension, being prepared to give a bit. Gentleness is a gift that takes more courage to receive than the impulse to violence. Gentleness is a desire to give space to the otherness of each other, to risk the inclusion of those with whom we struggle – and that will also include the struggle we have with the violence within ourselves. If we are to be gentle then we need to discover that it is possible for us not to be too hard on ourselves. It is said that when men and women come out as being gay the most homophobic person they need to convince is themselves. Maybe the things that we find most difficult about ourselves are the things that are essentially who we are – the things that are of the very essence of us. When I am angry about something, I am often more angry with myself for feeling like that. I do not want to consider myself an angry person. 'The Angry Woman' is such a powerful negative image. But I have to acknowledge I am angry. The call to be gentle is a call to be gentle with the essence of ourselves, to be accepting of our own identities. There is a lot of me that I do not really want to accept, that I would prefer to deny, to ignore rather than to change. I sense that if we are able to discover some integrity within ourselves then we will be enabled to embark upon the tough struggle towards inclusion within our communities. There is an old Celtic prayer hanging on our wall that begins, 'Be gentle when you touch bread ...'.

The loaves are still warm and release a last breath of steam as they break open. Tony's soup is ladled into bowls and the quantity does not diminish visibly in the pan. Jesus sat at table with a traitor, a sceptic and others who wanted to do their best but fell asleep or ran away when the going got tough. This is an important time to be together, whoever we are, sharing the same bread. This is a radically different encounter from that which is happening outside our door. This intention to include, the struggle we have to see each other within our humanity, the negotiation of space – even around a pan of soup, these things matter. We are trying to live in a different way – to work with the differences that confront us and stretch us to the very limits of our wisdom. We are trying to live out of the spaces between us – spaces that give us some focus on each others' faces. So maybe there is some sign of hope given by this small sign of contradiction. It is such a fragile thing. Maybe it is not enough, but at least it is a start.

To experience our experience can be confrontational, yet it can bring us to a new honesty. We can feel as though we are grinding to a halt, yet new life comes not by avoiding issues but by walking through them. Yes, we are confronted with those things that challenge us to the very essence of ourselves, yet our experience leads us to engagement not avoidance. Living out of our own questions is a turbulent process. How we live out of our anger is a life-and-death issue and easy answers are nothing but a diversion. In the meantime I want to continue being angry. I want to keep turning the tables on the loud mouths and the drugs pushers. I will continue to go sometimes to stand with Michael. I even resolve to try to find a way to tell Christians with whom I have a difference that 'My Jesus is not your Jesus' and try to accept that 'their Jesus' is Jesus too. What I am praying for here is the grace to stay angry – and to do so gently.

7

Eating

It is Easter Sunday. Upstairs in a small room a group of people are meeting for a meal. Actually it is breakfast and it is us. Some of the group (me in particular) are feeling a bit groggy. We had thought about meeting at dawn at the edge of the Mersey but decided to postpone 'dawn' until eight o'clock. Even so, for Marie 8 a.m. is the end of the night before. At the river the ferries were already chuntering into life. Herring gulls reeled around the Cunard buildings eddying like the water that swished around the landing stage. The Albert Dock is built on bales of cotton and rises imperceptibly with the incoming tide. Long talons of kelp and bladderwrack cling to the harbour wall. The clank of metal ropes against masts chimes as if church bells call the day into life.

Christ may have risen but the city has not risen. It is silent. The perfect proportions of the Georgian buildings stand assuredly but rather dishevelled – like elderly Miss Havishams – still anticipating their big moment. They have witnessed more confident times. Days of empire and the Queen Mary lying at anchor at the Pier Head. They have sheltered Irish immigrants huddling on their steps against wet westerly winds. Squeezed between them rise concrete city-centre 'dwellings'. Plastic sheets wave brashly from skimpily clad penthouses waiting for windows.

At the bandstand we have stood sheepishly, alone, wrapped in scarves and woolly mittens. Passing a chalice between us

Marie, still dreaming, takes a sip of wine and to the words 'the blood of Christ' uses the as-yet-unheard-of liturgical response 'cheers'. We break the bread. It is our bread, we have made it. We love it. Carole reads the story of the lakeside, how the disciples recognised Jesus at breakfast time by the water's edge. We nod, we know this story.

I have declined the offer of a lift feeling the need to walk. I make my way up through the town on my own. From the Liver Building where the griffins brood over the face of the river, I make my way up Water Street. At the Parish Church of Our Lady and St Nicholas, squeezed into a triangle of green, lying to the left of me, the verger is unlocking the door. St Nick's is a church with a long relationship with the lives of seafarers and their waiting families. I make my way past the town hall with its golden dome, where councillors struggle daily to give civic life a human face, and turn into Castle Street. I plod past the banks and solicitors' offices, turning left in front of the law courts where three bedraggled skate-boarders skim along the kerb as Victoria glowers from her monument. Past the shut doors of British Home Stores and the statue of the Moores brothers outside Littlewoods. The tills are resting in these shops that usually compete daily for their place on the high street. So many local people's livelihoods depend on this rivalry. I go on past Central Station where the platforms are deserted and the trains rest in their depot. Up the hill of Bold Street with its wrapping of shutters, concealing the windows adorned in anticipation for Monday's sales by tired assistants before they set off for home yesterday. Ahead of me lies the bomb-gutted carcase of St Luke's.

Upstairs in the bread kitchen the see-saw picture has been pinned into place. The paper child rises among rubbish in the park. During Easter Saturday the rainbow has been coloured in a spectrum of eccentric felt-pen shades. Toast is cooking and eggs, there are some enormous packets of cereal and a big jug of milk. The smell of coffee promises the caffeine desired to pull the struggling among us back to life.

When Jesus finally arrived back at the home of Mary, Martha and Lazarus there were all the symptoms of grief in the air, anger, disbelief, guilt, denial, tears, accusations, 'Lord, if only you had been here my brother would not have died.' It is a justifiable response in the face of death. It is a natural reaction to accuse the one whose promises have proved hollow, the world is charged with 'if onlys'. If only Michael's family had kept contact with him, if only Simon's rucksack had not been stolen, if only Penny's parents had let her be a girl, if only Col's father had discovered another way. If only young people came to church, if only the city council had a joined-up approach to homelessness, if only we could temper capitalism with compassion, if only we could learn to share the world's resources, if only we could find peace. Dying and living, they are wrapped up together. Seams of bereavement, of absence, of grief run through the seemingly solid rocks of our lives. We are shot through with loss. As the Psalmist says as he senses the Godlessness of his surroundings, 'Have they no understanding all those evildoers who devour my people as if eating bread, and never call to the Lord? They will be in dire alarm, for God is in the assembly of the righteous. Though you would frustrate the counsel of the poor, the Lord is their refuge. If only deliverance for Israel might come from Zion!' (Psalm 14:4–7). If only Jesus had been there Lazarus would not have died.

I am fearful for this city, despite its brave attempts to engage with its 2008 City of Culture status. I am anxious that we will end up with a plastic version of the place. A plastic version of the city is one that ignores the 'if onlys', where we begin to pretend being alive is simply about being clean, presentable and not causing a stink. Already the homeless guys are being politely swept off the streets; the symptoms of homelessness are being alleviated, but what about the roots? Poverty is complex. It is the result of the impoverishment of the inner city as money is pulled into the city centre. It is the outcome of policies concerning drug abuse – is it a criminal or a medical condition? It is the symptom of an asylum policy that makes people invisible. It is an outcome of globalisation where multinationals cause communities to be displaced or side-lined to follow economic trends. Regeneration can be a means of enlivening the fabric of a city, but what about its soul? Remaining alive is not simply being a moving, breathing body but making connections with the very essence of what makes us the 'I am' of ourselves. Who is calling the city into life by its own name?

Life and death are wrapped up together. We can stifle our visionaries with policy statements, embalm them with rules. We can cover over the bad smell of neglect, hide it away, make the unacceptable invisible. We can roll stones of good intentions in front of the deadly causes of poverty. Yes, but we may all be trapped by good intentions. We can become very tired of waiting for things to be different and cynical about what that difference is going to mean. In the face of big institutions and corporate power we can be stuck, abandoned, lost and angry. If only we knew what to do then we would do it, but the opposition is too weightily stacked against us. What on earth is the point of making bread, three loaves at a time, when the raising of our rent by absentee landlords could displace everybody in this street at a swipe. There can be a stand-off between death and life, Mary in the house and Lazarus in the tomb.

Maybe one symptom of this stand-off is the bureaucracy that locks good intentions in a gridlock of paperwork. Fundraising is now a task that requires the well-honed skills of creative mathematics, succinct prose and the ability to imagine virtual realities. Money comes our way but gets siphoned off by the system. It is important to be accountable but it is equally important to deliver. The intention of the funders may be to bring people a better life but the process by which change is delivered often proves too cumbersome for the small and vulnerable. Yet it is often the most fragile of organisations that are best equipped to be alongside those that are most at risk. Small organisations sense their own mortality, they live the struggle for survival daily, they know what it is like to face death and this makes them best equipped to offer life.

Death and life even in their proximity to each other can remain perpetually unaddressed. 'If you had been here my brother would not have died.' There is guilt in dying, as if it is failure, as if it can be helped. But death is the only inevitable thing, the only thing of which we can be sure. So we can live with a paralysis brought about by death's unaddressed inevitability. So too the inherited church lives out of such a paralysis. Death is seen as the end, the final triumph of evil over good, the end of the road. Imagine how it felt when the Methodist Central Hall became a casino; as a denomination we may be more petrified than most of our impending demise. It can feel as if God has sealed the church in with its own decay. We are no longer able to operate as previous generations have expected, but we pretend so that we can avoid facing our death. We will never be able to live until we acknowledge we are going to die.

You could feel sorry for Lazarus. Just when he thought the worst was over he was called back to do it all again. He stumbles out into his sister's unfinished grief, dazzled by the afternoon light penetrating his unbound eyes, into the bewildering realisation that death was something already conquered. The strange gift of this for him is that he will live the remainder of his days in the light of his dying.

When the bride with the brain tumour came to be married, knowing already the terminal nature of her illness, she was making such a statement about her life in the light of her death. There were tears and laughter. They were not sentimental tears, they were tears that faced the outcome of her illness and brought a huge determination to live every moment in its deepest intensity. She took her grandchildren to a special place in the park where they would be able to remember her later. They made bread together. They sang and partied and said some of those things that should have been shared years ago. It did not ease the grief or the parting, her family still had to let her go. Her limited days had an exquisite intensity about them. She showed us all in that short time what it might mean to have life in all its fullness. She was able to do this because she began to live in the light of death. The two were not opposites, they were part of the same picture, the way it is for all of us, the way it is meant to be. This is the point at which the 'if onlys' begin to pivot on their heels and become 'and yets'.

It is sensing our own fragility that brings us to this realisation sooner or later. That is why the most fragile among us are the ones who can often show us others the way. 'He will stink', this corpse of a man that has been dead and gone for four days. Maybe it is best to leave things alone. Michael stinks. No one really cares if he disappears. Unbelievably in this country we still have paupers' graves and the corpses of the poorest and kinless are put into unmarked graves in zipped-up body bags. Who cares when a homeless guy overdoses or a man with schizophrenia cuts his own wrists? Is it just an inevitable outcome of urban life? Who cares if traditional churches bite the dust? Is it just a consequence of secularisation and pluralism? Who cares if the city disintegrates? Is it just the sure result of urbanisation and capitalism? It is only when we experience the experience of our dying that we know what it is to be called into life. To be called out of our cycles of death and decay and find new life in regeneration, social inclusion and the unbinding of the Spirit of God.

Jesus has been accused of being absent when he was most needed. He has deliberately stayed away and now he is returning not only to his family of friends who are almost beyond speaking to him but he is also returning to a place so fraught with danger that he will face his accusers and be crucified. It was a ludicrous decision. Lazarus was dead and buried, Jesus was in fear of his life, and yet he turns on his heel and returns. Jesus says to Lazarus, 'Come out,' and he stumbles back into life, still wrapped up with the trappings of death. 'Untie him', Jesus says, 'and let him go.' Life is a calling. Life is only a given for now, this moment, this present intersection of time and eternity. Life is the result of this breath that I breathe now. Life is the inhalation of the present moment, the consciousness of the now of my own body. Only because there is an inevitable death is there a present moment. As we experience the experience of our mortality so we can experience the experience of the series of 'nows' that give us life. Our only vocation is to live, to live our lives tenderly, gloriously, gently, to be alive. God calls us to live. We can only claim our lives if we can first claim our death. In the light of our death we can choose life.

I predict that the traditional ways of most inherited churches will die. And yet the Spirit of God is not dead, it continues to connect those who are prepared to look death in the face and dare to live anyway. It is time for fresh nourishment. The spirit of life causes sparks between contrasting people in laughter, anger and love. Facing the death of the church is a deep grief to those of us who have known its life. I have been nurtured by Methodism and my nonconformist blood runs very deeply in my veins. And yet, I need to face up to the absence of a strong living body of believers. I must let the old familiar wrappings of religion pass away. Hard though it is I sense that it is only if the faithful live in the light of our death will we find the way for the church to come back to life.

In this kitchen we have worked hard on understanding the bread that we make. We have noticed that the ingredients have resonances within the gospels, yeast, oil, salt, water, flour, honey. We have come to experience the process as a means by which stories unfold and memories are liberated. We have also found the spaces within the process to let God pray within us and bring us into a new way of relating. We have struggled with the tensions between inclusion and safety. We have discovered the fragility of the bread community, so easily broken, so easily consumed, so fragmented and risky. But there is more to life than this and sometimes we have forgotten that all the discovery of the wonder of bread is so that we can enjoy being alive.

A student was with me on placement. She was studying the Eucharist. Her question was whether the bread church was an 'authentic eucharistic community'. She was diving into all kinds of learned tomes that helped her understand eucharistic theology, the tradition of the church, the hallmarks of Christian community, the liturgies and doctrines that would help her discern what was authentic. She was doing pretty well when she suddenly had a crisis. She rang me late one night, 'Barbara, where is the wine?' This is not such an easy question for a Methodist to answer. The wine that came to my mind was the alcoholic extravaganza that was being imbibed in Wood Street. We are situated in the middle of the club and pub area of the city centre. Everywhere is awash with wine of one kind or another. Where was our wine? I flannelled an unsatisfactory answer and went away to think.

Where is the wine in a community such as ours? It was Col who began to answer the question for us. She suddenly said, 'When we put water into our bread – then it's like that water becomes wine.' Yes, of course, we add water and it is transformed into wine in the joy and thanksgiving of our community. And if that sounds rather pious and dull then I need to tell you that we have some pretty riotous parties and can laugh so long and loud that our sides ache for days. That is not because we are ignoring the deep, dark, serious issues that confront us at every turn; on the contrary, it is because in the facing of them we have begun to face our death and decided to live anyway. A survivor of sexual abuse has faced death, and someone who is kicked by passers-by as he sleeps on a doorstep has faced death, and an asylum-seeker held at knife point in a car has faced death, and someone whose marriage has crumpled in their hands has faced death. I am employed by a church that faces death and may not be able to continue funding this project. We live in a city that has faced death, in bombing raids, prejudice and at the unscrupulous hands of property developers. And yet in the light of all that we want to live. Not just exist in some half life that denies both our dying and our living but real life, full life, the kind of life that makes a difference, continues to battle with injustice and, without denying any of that struggle, has fun.

So, Marie's response to the offered chalice may not be as inept as it at first appeared. Maybe the response to the realisation of death and vulnerability and brokenness is to receive the broken Christ and to respond 'cheers' – albeit not in a flippant unthinking way but as a response that comes from a deep-down sense of being called into life. The offering of life is not only a responsibility and a commitment – it is the promise of joy. Living in the light of our dying is a calling to look at ourselves, if you like, through the other end of the telescope. It is the unbinding of our imaginations into the realisation that we have faced the worst and all is not lost. If we live our lives from beginning to end we may view it as an incremental journey where we are valued by the things and experiences we have accumulated along the way. If we live our lives in the light of our death then we know that there will be an ultimate time when we have nothing, we have experienced nothing, we have faced being nothing and nothing holds any fear any more. In this way we are able to shed the accumulated result of our life's choices and live out of a place where we are free not to be bound by choice. If we can see from the perspective of having nothing it shows us the 'everything' of being present to the experience of being alive now. Experiencing the experience of death and to find within it the experience of life is the beginning of living in a new way, an unsmothered way, a place where we are free to breathe.

This, the bread has taught me and, together with the wine, brings me to a new encounter with the Eucharist. Bread made and broken, wine shared and poured, fragile struggling bodies, fertile, celebrating, laughing, joyful encounters. We need both to be flesh-and-blood people. Bread and wine become the elements of a new way of being as individuals and community.

Through them we come to see Eucharist not so much as an event but as a way of relating. The way, as with the bread, is that of gathering, remembering, confessing, holding, breaking, transforming, thanking, sharing and departing. This bread-making process has shown us the liturgical shape of our every-day lives. It has demonstrated the possibility of experiencing lives of the greatest trauma and the greatest gratitude. Not, first one and then the other, but both together, in a real communion of experience, real presence, the totally transformative reality of the totally ordinary. The 'I am' of the bread.

We have finished our cornflakes and have moved on to a large solid chocolate Easter egg. Someone is encouraging Col to sing. She does not require a lot of encouragement, she has a brilliant voice and can sing almost any request thrown her way. If you do not know that Col was forbidden to sing when she was a child then you do not quite perceive the miracle that is happening here. She sings 'It's Raining Men' and this causes a lot of merriment from various members of our community representing a wide range of sexual orientations. We are mid song when the doorbell rings and we see Michael and John asking to come in. We are aware that we have forgotten them as we have been busy gorging ourselves on chocolate. If you did not know how it is for the pair of them you would not see the miracle of them coming inside to sit at the table and drink tea with us. John has a bandage around his ear. He has been in a fight. They eat, speak little and fall asleep. After a while we tune into the radio. We have been recorded for Radio 4's *Food Programme*. We hush as we listen to ourselves on the radio. Here is a voice we recognise – it is Penny reading a poem and talking to the presenter about 'being different'. If you did not know the story of Penny's struggle to find her own voice, a woman's voice, then you would have missed the miracle here. We all cheer! It is because she is different that Penny has been interviewed over and above the more conventional bakers. Penny has her voice – Radio 4 on Easter Sunday. These are miracles of life.

Dying and living, they are wrapped up together and it is living from the perspective of dying that gives us the possibility, like God, of making something out of nothing. That is why it was such a gift to me to be sent to a place where the church felt it had lost everything – the sale of Liverpool Central Hall was charged with grief, there was a ten-year wait before this little community appeared. It is hard for us to wait outside a shut door and realise that the opening to a fresh start might lie in a different direction. And yet if we stand and wait within all our grief and despair there will be signs of new life – albeit small quirky signs – just as in the depths of winter there are hints of spring. And here is an amazing thing. This bread church of which I am a part is so authentically Methodist that it makes me smile. It is small, it believes that the Gospel should be in the hands of the poorest, it has a social conscience and a profound sense of God's grace. This new body of believers is recognisable by its family of origin. We are of the same blood. Experiencing the experience of our dying has brought us life.

All around us in the city there are such signs of coming to life. The city council perseveres with regeneration and the YMCA is moving to a new city-centre site. Simon has been at work for a week and Michael has come inside for breakfast. Not everyone bursts into life like Lazarus but there are signs of stirring. Resurrection can be a long, slow, fragile process. Even four days feels like eternity when you sense something is lost for ever. Mary and Martha had to wait a long time with their 'if onlys', they had to wait to the point that death was certain, past any hope of recovery, past any possibility of their friend being who he had promised to be. And yet, when Jesus returned and Lazarus was raised to life, they were given not only their brother but a whole new way of living – a way of living in the face of dying.

Col's notion that we mix water in with our bread and it becomes wine in some wonderfully transformative way is a profound insight. Water into wine is such a life-giving metaphor for the way the ordinary can be transformed into the celebratory. I sit back and listen to our Easter party. Tony, Carole and Marie are falling about laughing. They are remembering the moment when a rather dishevelled woman rang the doorbell to come to the tai chi class that was meeting in our middle room. Tony had answered the bell and announced to the assembled bread-makers, 'Some woman's come to practise karma sutra in the middle room!' Beneath the joke is the delight within the community that Tony is now part of the group of people that answers the bell. He talks of 'my church' and his journey as a recovering alcoholic is one in which we all share. He has stories to tell of our very first conversations on the street five years ago. He has taught me so much about myself and what makes life important. A few weeks ago we had been to Llandudno to talk with a group of churches there. It was the first time Tony had been through the Mersey tunnel by car. When we returned to the city centre late at night I dropped him back to the YMCA where he has lived on and off for the last ten years. 'It's really good to be home,' he said as he jumped out of the car. This kind of thankfulness is a gift that has come to us through the breaking of the fragile bread and the sharing of the dancing wine. It is the delight of eucharistic living.

Bread and wine together are what makes this sense of thanksgiving. Bread has reminded us of the fragile, vulnerable nature of our lives. Wine returns us to engagement with our embodied selves, to live the physicality of our being. One day I would like to dance the Eucharist. This connection between bread and wine reminds me of the need to live our lives with some integrity. Bread-making is a physical activity. Your arms will ache and your shoulders be exercised in the kneading of dough. It is an emotional exercise. You will tell stories and thump the lump of mixture as anger and frustrations are transformed into physical movement. It is a spiritual exercise as the bread reminds us of our dependence on the earth and the created world, each other and our relationships. These are not separate things, they are all aspects of what it means for any one of us to be a human being. Body, mind and spirit are integral parts of the 'I am of ourselves'. If our emotions are in turmoil then we will find it hard to pray, if our bodies ache then we will struggle to concentrate. The holiness of bread is that it holds all these aspects of us in a creative tension. That is not to say that any one of us is complete in ourselves – I do not believe in a quest for holiness that can be equated with perfection. On the contrary, bread opens a window on the idea that we thrive when we are held in a creative dynamic between our physical, emotional and spiritual needs. To be holy is not the ultimate goal of someone who has had all other needs satisfied. On the contrary, it is the result of seeing ourselves as incomplete, struggling human beings who are living within a mixture of experiences. To experience our experience of deep, nuanced, contradictory, struggling, joyful, flawed humanity is the medium of holiness. I am coming to realise that holiness is not so much a state to be achieved but a way to live.

This possibility of holiness is as much of an insight for the city as for the individual. We cannot wait for our physical environment to be sorted before we address our emotional needs and our spiritual growth is part of the same equation. That is why it is often the people who have the least physically who make the biggest contribution to holiness. Facing our death and living anyway is a spiritual decision. 'What does anyone gain by winning the whole world at the cost of destroying himself?' What does it gain a city if it becomes a City of Culture and loses its own identity? This is holy ground, not when it is sanctified and safe but when it is messily alive.

Easter is not an answer to everything, it is the greatest of all questions. How are life and death mixed up together? How can we discover that living and dying are not opposites but stand alongside us as we experience our experience? How can we live out of our questions with the perspective of our death, but go on believing in life? Living out of the questions of dying brings us firmly to the question of being alive.

And what of the whole earth, the earth that is only holy when the whole of creation has room to breathe? We can dream of a time when economics and politics are mindful of and accountable to humanity and the ecologists are able to protect the earth's lungs, when the estuary with its bladder-wrack and gulls and the gutters with their rosebay willowherb and moss are given their due honour. We could dare to believe in a time when the architect searches for beauty as well as utility and there is a sense that the city can be acclaimed for its creativity as well as its function, when we can discover the city environment to be as much a place of growth and flourishing as the countryside with which it must struggle for mutual respect. This is a dream, I know. But it is a waking dream.

8

Giving

John is dead. He was taken into hospital last night and died of septicaemia. He was 31 years old and his system was shot. I never knew his second name. In the absence of relatives there is to be a collection at the *Big Issue* office to buy some flowers. Michael is trying to sell extra magazines today to make a contribution to the fund.

A woman at a church meeting last night asked me how we knew our church was a real church and not just a social club. 'How do you evangelise?' she pushed me for an answer. I did not respond particularly well. Maybe I should go back and invite her to stand beside Michael as he sells the *Big Issue* today. See if she thinks that is a social club kind of activity. (Oh God, turn my anger to gentleness.) As we make bread we are more aware than usual of the temporary nature of who we are. Here today and gone tomorrow, there is a fickle transience to existence. What could you possibly say to Michael today?

Experiencing the experience of emptiness, of desolation, of abandonment, of senselessness cannot provoke any other response except the experience of emptiness, desolation, abandonment and senselessness. There is no answer at this time, no word, no creation, no resurrection, no incarnation, no safety, nothing. I defy the shortcut to an answer; there is no response other than to live the question.

I would like to say that the resurrection of Jesus is the end of the story, the happy ending, the answer to all our ills, the 'I rest my case' of the theological argument, but I cannot. After resurrection, new life, insight, revelation, transformation, there is another day. The day after the resurrection when the disciples believed yet still doubted. That is how it is with us today too. We believe in life but when we wake up in the morning John is dead. This is not a fairy tale kind of story – where Pinocchio becomes a real boy and everyone lives happily ever after. This is a real life story where there is always another chapter, another dilemma, another way of looking at things. We find an empty tomb but we return to the garden, we see the Lord but we confront our own alienation, we have been blind and now we see, yet only through dark glasses, mirror images, hints and rumours of an elusive God.

John will not have his own grave. He will have a pauper's funeral and there will be no members of his family present – mainly because no one knows if he had any family. And anyway, would the next of kin be interested now? He was not an easy man. He was a drug addict and a thief. He was consumed by his own addictions and his fragile mental health. But we will miss him and while the poor will always be with us one way and another, there is something of John that will not be replaced. He has been part of who we are.

Mary said in desolation, 'They have taken the Lord out of the tomb . . . and we do not know where they have laid him' (John 20:3). How familiar is that cry when everything is lost. They have taken it all away and I am desolate. There is such a desperate unfixable-ness to the human situation. However hard we try and however long we work we cannot make everything right here. We experience our own powerlessness at every turn. As Jesus from the cross quotes the Psalmist when he cries in his own desolation, 'My God, my God, why have you forsaken me?', so we are left within our own questions crying out, 'Why are you so far from saving me, so far from heeding my groans?' (Psalm 22:1).

As we make bread today we are subdued. When we have nothing, not even anything to say, then all we can be is the messed-up human beings we all are. Like the dough at its stickiest the only choice is to live the mess. I look around the table at the morning's bakers: Ahmed, Tony, Terry, Heather. Col has bad memories that mean she finds it difficult to knead the dough, but she is making coffee. At prayer time we remember John, conscious of our powerlessness and the weather turning colder by the day. The only thing that makes living the mess easier is that we are together in the same mess. We are not a community with answers but a community that is trying to live our questions.

Jesus asks, 'Why have you forsaken me?' Mary asks, 'Where is the Lord?' Thomas asks, 'How do you know this is Jesus?' The gardener asks, 'Why are you weeping?' And we ask, 'Why did it have to be like this for John?' We ask hard questions about our city – whether regeneration is actually helping us, whether we trust people in authority, whether there is a way to improve relationships between commerce and the powerless. We question government policy on asylum, the relationship between cities and the countryside, and our solidarity with those who are unfed. We question whether there is a future for the church, whether Christianity has any mileage in it any more, whether God has abandoned us or is simply an illusion for the weak-minded. Like Mary we stand in perplexity within our questions and it is only because we choose to live out of these questions that I believe we can claim we are people of faith. We have faith not because we know the answers but because we are prepared to continue to stand in our not-knowing, because we do not know why the tomb is empty, because we wonder how this up-to-our-elbows mess can ever be bread.

Experiencing the experience of our own questions without fear is what makes this community a church rather than a sect. Sects brainwash followers into a mindset that cannot challenge the authority of their self-appointed leaders, they coerce by fear, and they do not let people leave. I believe that one significant hallmark of our authenticity is that we continue to doubt. Thank God for Thomas who wanted to touch the wounds, to see with his own eyes before he would believe in the risen Jesus. He gave all subsequent disciples permission to live their own questions, to be sceptical about certainties, neat solutions and a 'fix it' formula for faith. If we are without doubts there is no need to believe, there is dogma rather than faith, closed minds rather than open hearts. God save the church from followers who have no doubts.

So, like Mary, it is not possible for us to cling to the certainty of a risen Lord. We can only experience our experience of faith at the moment it comes to us. Faith cannot be wrapped up, sealed in or nailed down. It is a living, breathing, enigmatic, perplexing encounter with something we neither understand nor possess. It is the surprising meeting with an unanswered question and the call to let the encounter challenge every assumption we want to hold about life, death, relationships, creation and ethics. Experiencing the experience of faith is to be given life in all its perplexing fullness. It is the call to live with our own name and out of our own questions.

The bread is in carrier bags ready to be taken all over the place. Tony is taking some to the *Big Issue* office. A gift is his way of saying that he stands in solidarity with the struggle. We do not sell the bread but give it away, considering it to be a gift to us in the first place. It is a surprisingly subversive thing to do and it does not pay the rent. Giving the gift of bread is something that calls into question the assumption of commercialism as the only way. In this small thing we stand as counter-signs. It is a risky thing. It calls us into the reality of only being here for today and not worrying too much about what the future will hold for us. We recognise that we are not building a church for eternity but rather trying to be faithful in the reality of today. That is quite a wobbly thing. Personally I would prefer to know that my stipend will be paid next year but no one can promise that. We have to keep our nerve.

In this process of keeping our nerve we must also resist the desire to shut the door and retrench. It has proved too great a temptation for many churches who have preferred to secure the fabric of their buildings rather than risk further encounter with things and people they do not understand. This is the way of death. To live out of our questions continues to call us into risky encounters. Encounters where we have no idea what the outcome will be. Just as bread has been an unexpected gift to us, so faith is an unexpected gift. Faith comes as a gift. We do not know why we have it but it calls us to be generous. Faith is not a commodity to be peddled with some evangelical hard-sell; it is a gift to be shared, like loaves and fishes among a multitude. The gift of faith is not so much an exchange of truth from the powerful to the disempowered but rather a connection of human beings within the dilemma of our own humanity. It is a to-and-fro thing. Like the gardener, standing with Mary in the not understanding, like the disciples trying to believe behind a locked door.

As someone who is trying to become a Christian I still find the need to read the bible and say my prayers, to check out my beliefs in a community and with reference to others. I need to have a conversation with those whom I trust and whose insights will differ from mine. This might be in an everyday conversation or through reading and study. In this way I hold my questions alongside the tradition, just as in this writing I have found connection with the gospel of John and with the Psalms. I need to monitor my own power: am I doing what I should be doing, am I relating in ways that are constructive and freeing? I need to trust this process and not be afraid of the things that might appear dangerous to my beliefs. If what I believe is authentic and true to a God of love then I have nothing to fear. Honest doubt and true faith are not opposites. They are the hallmarks of our intentions.

Faith is not so much something to be believed but something to be lived. It would have been completely pointless if the first disciples had simply believed in the resurrection of Jesus and died with their belief. There were implications to believing. It made a difference to what they did next. It made them take the risk of living their lives in a different way, of engagement with structures, powers and individuals. They were fired up with a desire to make a difference. They had to put their bodies where their beliefs were. This was not a particularly comfortable undertaking. It involved standing up and living out of their convictions. It brought a lot of trouble then and it brings a lot of trouble now. We are not on a journey of understanding but on a journey into life. Not so much thinking something different but being something different. It is a whole-body thing. That is why it is a lifetime's quest. Sometimes we will get there and sometimes we will be way off the mark. Towards the end of St John's gospel Simon Peter says, 'I am going fishing.' The others reply, 'We will go with you', and they went out in the boat and caught nothing at all. That is the risk, the risk of solidarity in the perplexity of it all. Not only does Peter catch nothing but everyone catches nothing. They are together in the same boat with the same experience of nothing.

At sea, caught between believing and not believing, the disciples know it is best to be together. At first light an unknown figure on the beach suggests they throw out the net to starboard – experienced fishermen would have known better than this. They think they know how to catch fish and yet they are prepared to listen to the surprising suggestion of a stranger standing on the lake's edge. The haul of fish may be simply a good catch but we perceive it to be a sign. The overwhelming catch calls them back to land. 'It is the Lord,' says the disciple whom Jesus loves. Peter goes first. Whoever heard of a naked man putting on his cloak before jumping into a lake? It is not a very sensible impulse. Better to leave the cloak until the others arrive with it, keep it dry so that it will still provide some warmth. Peter believes but he only half believes. He believes he can walk on water but he puts his cloak on first. It is only when the rest of the company arrive with the night's catch that they begin to see that the bread of Jesus and the fish of their joint struggle make a life-giving meal. 'Who are you?'

they ask, knowing already it is the Lord. The question, the half belief, the gathering of a wet cloak, the fire, the recognition, the giving of bread ... that is the story.

Tony puts on his coat and gets ready to take his bread. Simon is at work. Ahmed has already been delivering leaflets and needs to go now to the library where he is returning a Farsi video. Col has a meeting with a group of male survivors, Heather has a counselling class, Carole is going to her store chaplaincy at John Lewis, I have a meeting with the city-centre ecumenical team. We set out in a variety of different directions. 'Do not cling to me,' Jesus says to Mary, 'but go to my brothers,' and I would like to add 'and sisters'.

An unhealthy church thinks that the object of being there is to be there. It is not just survivors who need to know where the exits lie, all of us need to understand that faith is not a trap but an opening, a two-way door. A genuine church is one that people leave. We form these encounters as equals falling into step side by side with whoever we meet. It is not possible to be a store chaplain and profess to know all the answers. Carole will face some hard dilemmas as she engages with the work-force at John Lewis. There are sharp issues brought into focus through the plan for the store to move to a new development site in the middle of town. This development will disrupt one of Liverpool's longest-established retail outlets. The city centre will move and other stores may well feel grounded in the process. Heather is listening to elderly people as they share some of their struggle. She needs to learn the patience and acceptance of the counsellor and that will cause her to face some of her unresolved issues. Listening is a hard job. I must engage with the struggle of the ecumenical team. We are friends but we are often neglectful of each other, more inter-ested in our own corners than in the bigger picture of what it means to be the church here.

At Simon's job interview the woman put his CV to one side and asked how he usually spent his time. He came back glee-fully, telling us that not only had he spent half an hour telling the woman all about 'his bread church' but also that he got the job. She had apparently been amazed that someone went to church and liked it! We do not usually go around with the intention of speaking to all and sundry about our church. It is more that it simply tends to come into conversations on its own. Around the kitchen table the gift of bread might prompt the conversation, but more often there is an uninvited interest that draws us in. How the word gets spread is a bit of a mystery, and the intention is not that we should go and preach so that people will come to church. The intention is to live the way of encounter that we are learning around the bread table in other contexts. It is about being genuine to the process we are discovering and to go on meeting people in their humanity wherever we find ourselves, to go on living out of our own questions wherever we encounter the questions. The intention is not to form a church but to be people who desire others to love their confusing, troubled, wonderful lives as deeply as we do. This is not the imposition of guilt and obligations by the powerful upon the unsuspecting, but rather the connection of equals with insights and experiences within our common yet disparate humanity. The point of faith is not to be religious but to be faithful.

When Jesus said, 'I am the bread', I believe he was making a whole-body statement the depth of which I am only just beginning to grasp. Yes, he was talking about the sustenance of people – body, mind and soul. He was talking about nourishment, of being a source of energy and wholeness. He was also indicating his own brokenness and the fragile nature of our survival. He was pointing to a quest for justice, for sharing, for generosity. He was giving disciples a visible and tangible memory of himself among them. Not only that, but he was connecting with his people through history, from the manna in the wilderness to the bread eaten by David on the Sabbath, through the temptations in the wilderness to this tentative group of followers around a table. I come to see that he was indicating a way of being, a way of encounter, pauses, listening, speaking and deep silence. He was engaging the physical and emotional part of our humanity, drawing us together within ourselves and among ourselves. He was talking in signs and metaphor but he was also indicating the real presence of his incarnation. 'I am the bread' is an existential statement – this is me, Jesus with you. You are seen, known, accompanied and loved.

So, the hallmarks of church are sacramental hallmarks – the outward signs of inward realities. There are the oldest and deepest sacraments of baptism and Eucharist, but there are also the sacraments of creativity, physicality and right relations. The insight that simple things are sacred, even ordinary bread as it is broken and shared among us. This bread is sacred because it is ordinary. It is holy because it has been made lovingly among a community that struggles to be authentic and faithful. This church is very, very far from ideal. We really battle with our desire to be both inclusive and safe. There are people here whom it is extremely hard to tolerate and there are some whom we have failed to welcome. We all get tired, confused and irritable. We are beset with questions, often stuck for words, feel powerless and useless, but at this moment, around this table, we are alive in a way that is a deep mystery and intensely real. This is how it is.

The gospel of St John ends with a conversation between Peter and Jesus. This has not been an easy relationship. The question Peter is asked three times is 'Do you love me?' Some say that Jesus asks three times because Peter denied Jesus three times. Whatever the reason for the threefold questioning it does not seem to reassure Peter; on the contrary he gets hurt and sad that it is necessary to ask three times 'Do you love me?' Each time he replies 'Yes, Lord, you know that I love you,' and after each response there is a command to tend the sheep and the lambs. The gospel-writer is very clear that this command is one that will lead to trouble – to the untimely execution of Peter in later life. Following Jesus, for Peter, is no easy call.

Giving

Like Peter we are continually dependent on the process of starting again, of being reinstated, of having another go. Being loved is the way in which we sense that we are valued and our lives considered worth living. That is why loving each other is worth the struggle, so that we can be signs to each other that we can begin again, even from where we are now. Jesus said to Peter, go and tend and love and feed those people that I would tend and love and feed. You, Peter, fumbling idiot that you are, are the one who can best signify what the church is about. Peter, the all-or-nothing follower, had to learn that following Jesus was going to be a lifetime's struggle to work it out, walking on water without being wrapped in the security of a cloak. Hopes, ideas, insights, longings were all changed, transfigured, re-configured as the story was lived. It is about the process of feeding and loving and tending because, unlikely though it seems in our present confused and messed-up state, we are able to be forgiven and reinstated. Not because we are powerful but because it still hurts when we are asked to love each other.

As we leave we pass Michael on the step. He is miserable and cold. Tony takes down a cup of tea with four sugars and a banana. There is someone new at the pitch outside the station, a man just demobbed from the army and unable to settle to civilian life. Outside Littlewoods a group of shop assistants chatter while a fire engine checks the store for hazards. Above us the gulls circle and cry. A mother with twins stands to listen to the man with the cardboard guitar as he sings a tuneless song and collects small change. Yoko Ono's photographs hang from drooping banners from the lamp-posts declaring 'Your mother is beautiful'. Tides of people move up Church Street intent on bargains and a cup of tea and an 'I shouldn't really' cake. A young woman on a mobile phone narrowly avoids walking into a lamppost. We do not bring God to this city, Carole, Tony, Heather and I. If God were dependent on us bringing God to the city then we would all be sunk. Resurrection means that God is not confined by human expectations. Mission is already happening, the spirit blows where it wills, there is life in abundance on offer here. Our calling is to go on believing that God is already here, among the people. Mission is not so much a process of us bringing the truth but of being equipped to recognise the truth when we see it – the reality of God at large among the shoppers, workers and tourists. God, out and about, praying within the most unlikely people, always ahead, always unknowable, always uncatchable, always enigmatic, yet somehow recognisable in moments of connection and surprise.

Do we love God? How can we? How do we love that which is essentially unknowable? God is a mystery to us, beyond our comprehension, the ultimate unanswerable question. Like Peter we stand perpetually in the not understanding, saying we love someone who is beyond our reach. And like Peter we are called only to love the sheep and lambs in whose company we live our days. We are not called to be the judges but the lovers of the humanity of others and indeed of ourselves. That job is big enough for anyone. It is both simple and immensely costly, it takes us to the limit of our understanding and beyond to a place where there can only be perplexity, wonder, incredulity and insight. We love God only by living our lives, every moment, every screwed up moment, until we are called into a place beyond comprehension. A place of relationship.

Terry may have learning difficulties but he does not have believing difficulties. He is always first into the quiet room at lunchtime and always keen to light a candle and say his prayers. Terry has been watching a programme on the TV about the Titanic. He told me about it. I said, 'Really, Terry, was it an interesting programme?' He said, 'Yes, it sank.' Terry sees the obvious things that we in our seemingly sophisticated worlds overlook. When I came back from sabbatical a few months ago it was Terry who gave me a big hug and said, 'I missed you,' and when one of our community was taxing beyond belief it is Terry who said, 'I like him.' Terry reminds us that the way of faith is profoundly simple. It is not about learning, knowledge or qualifications, it is about simply seeing the world in its wonder and, despite everything, considering it to be lovable.

In the beginning, out of the silence before creation, the word of God was spoken, spoken in person by a companion to humanity. I have a million questions around whether this is true or real, or if it makes any difference at all, yet there seems to be a connection with a living word, a companionable word, a struggling, questioning word that gives life a different perspective. We can speak of doors and shepherds and lights and vines and resurrection and life and bread in a new way because of that experience. Through this it becomes conceivable that we can experience the experience of a new possibility. It is an experience of hope. Not a blind optimism but a struggling realism in which we can go on looking for a new relationship, a new companionship, a new intentionality, a new discourse. We can view our city and our world and our own routine of everyday encounters with new eyes because of this mandate to love one another. We can see the perennial unsolved dilemmas of poverty with a depth of compassion because there is a solidarity in the struggle of engagement. We can understand our own value systems and priorities differently if we live in the light of our own dying. We can live the mysterious confusion of existence with a new courage because surprising things can happen and we no longer need to rely on our own limited understanding. Will our deaths be unmarked like Peter and John? Will we be put into an unnamed grave like Jesus and John? Will we be lost in the mists of eternity? Like Peter and Jesus and John that is the risk we take. Like Peter and John we are called to live out of these questions. But yet, in all this mixed-up, muddling confusion of being human beings here, now and somewhere else, there has been just the slightest hint of another way.

I am making bread. There is a warm smell of yeast bubbling enthusiastically with the honey in the jug. I write my initials in the flour with the oil. Then three spoons of salt disappear into the bowl. 'Don't you ever get tired of making bread?' someone asks. Truthfully I can answer, 'No'. It always fills me with excitement as I begin to pummel the glutinous mixture. The salt stings my hands. My fingers stick together. 'You have to go on believing in bread. You have to believe it knows it's going to be bread.' It does. Yeast and salt, oil and honey, warm water and malted flour combine to become elastic and smooth. They give each other life, texture, warmth and identity. Bread is full of wonder.

And so is the church of which I am a part. The 'bread church' working out what it means to be a Christian community around the making, shaping and sharing of bread. I look around the table. Here is a wonder-full community of odd bods like myself. We have wandered here from many different experiences with a variety of different motives. Simon used to sell the *Big Issue*, Tony still does. Col had 'sacked the church' and stumbled on us by accident. Penny is transgendered and has brought a number of people with mental health issues. Terry lives in a house run by the Independent Living Alliance. There is a student or two, Harry who is two years old and Ahmed who is seeking asylum. Some of this community are gay and have never felt really welcome in a church before. Some have been so abused that they have never felt safe anywhere, least of all in church. Others work and come to make bread to relax or think. This is the wonder of it.

In the beginning was the word but in the end there was an edgy relationship: Ahmed and Col and Penny, Peter and Jesus and all the others who have found the table-turning joy of being with each other. We are learning the challenge of being different, annoying, joyful, troubled and optimistic human beings. We are trying to trust the process of becoming what God intends us to be in the company of strangers. Learning to be companions, friends together, making bread.

More than that, this bread church has caused me to return to the gospels and re-examine what they might mean in a community such as this. How can we talk of salvation or holiness or Eucharist in such a way that it makes sense here? This is a challenge for me as I work alongside this mixed-up bread community. In reality it is the challenge for all people who still consider faith might be worth exploring – with Tony and Michael, with Ahmed and Col. Mysteriously each one of us is called into our own lives, into our own struggles, anger, joy, dancing and death. All we are doing is making bread, this little community of strange friends, mixing, kneading, waiting, rising, cooling, sharing, enjoying, leaving. This is how I am, how we all are, somewhere else.

Baskets

The rhythm of the week goes around. People gather, engage, tell stories, leave. Bread is made, broken, shared. Like life at times there can seem to be a relentless cycle of the days with little to show for it. And the church? Sunday by Sunday it takes bread and shares it and the offertory dwindles and people are tired. And we can look at each other like the disciples and shrug our shoulders and say, 'We haven't even got enough to feed ourselves let alone others, send everyone home.' That is the point, the very point at which the loaves and fishes appeared. So little among so many, but at the end of the day there were twelve baskets over.

The story of the bread church may feel as though it has gone round in a circle. So what that there is a group of people in the middle of Liverpool making a handful of loaves? The church is in decline and it feels so often that it would be better if we all went home. And we have hurt so many for so long, and hurled stones at each other, and missed the point, banged people who differ on the head with doctrine and failed to recognise the divine spirit in each other. There is little wonder that people of integrity have called us hypocrites.

That is why I want to say 'Yes, but'. Yes, Christians have missed the point. We have missed the signs and wonders because we have considered that we have had to feed the people single-handed rather than accept the gift of the giver. And the giver in this case is a little boy with a packed lunch, but it could as easily be an asylum-seeker with no name or a home-less guy with no bed or a feisty Glaswegian who says 'My Jesus is not your Jesus', or a woman celebrating her new body, or a lonely guy lost in his memories. At the end of the day, bread is made and shared among five thousand people but there are basketfuls left over. The pieces are gathered, nothing is wasted and there is enough to go to all the tribes and nations.

It was after the bread was shared that people began to make claims about Jesus, 'Surely this is the prophet . . .' They had the experience and they looked back to their tradition and their Scripture and they reasoned that there was something going on here that pointed to a different way, a way of simple gen-erosity and engagement with need. In this way also the bread church does not choose to launch out on its own. We have no desire at all to form a new church. We can see the traditional hallmarks of church reworked here as we share the weekly liturgy of gathering, listening, confessing, listening to the Scriptures, sharing the bread and wine and going away again. We have seen with new eyes that the word that was spoken in the beginning is a creative word and that having the courage to experience our experience will not close us down but open us up to new possibilities for growth.

When we experience the experience of our lives, when we begin to live out of our own questions and when we receive the gift of bread then maybe we also will ask, 'Who is this giver who has taken such small, ordinary things and named them holy?'